ARMY
OF THE
DAWN

PREPARING FOR THE GREATEST EVENT OF ALL TIME

RICK JOYNER

MorningStar Publications

ARMY OF THE DAWN

Army of the Dawn
by Rick Joyner
Copyright ©2015
Trade Size Edition

Distributed by MorningStar Publications, Inc.,
a division of MorningStar Fellowship Church
375 Star Light Drive, Fort Mill, SC 29715

www.MorningStarMinistries.org
1-800-542-0278

Original cover artwork by Bill Osborne. www.BillOsborne.com. Used by permission.

Cover and Layout Design: Kandi Evans and Michael R. Carter

ISBN— 978-1-60708-636-9; 1-60708-636-0

For a free catalog of MorningStar Resources, please call 1-800-542-0278

Table of Contents

CHAPTER ONE

A New Day

A new day will soon dawn over the whole earth. It is a day of healing, reconciliation, and restoration. It will heal every wound and reconcile everyone to their Creator and to one another. Ultimately, it will restore the earth to the Paradise it was originally created to be.

We have not come to the end of the world, but to a new beginning for the world. The emerging generation will be part of the greatest transition there has ever been on the earth. This is one of the greatest honors, but it will also be one of the greatest challenges. To navigate through these times, the world will be sent some of its greatest prophets and spiritual leaders of the age. These are the ones spoken of since the eighth generation from Adam.

The Prophetic Week

To understand these days we must know the base point in prophetic stages that all times are measured against—the biblical prophetic week. The Apostle Peter made an important statement for understanding biblical prophecy when he said: **"But, beloved, do not forget this one thing, that with the Lord one day is as a thousand years, and a thousand years as one day" (II Peter 3:8 NKJV).**

For him to say **"do not forget this one thing"** gives emphasis to just how important this is to understand. It is important to understand that when the Lord speaks of a day, it is often a one thousand year period. This is consistent in biblical prophecy. Using the genealogies in Scripture, we can determine that the Bible covers seven thousand years of history, or seven prophetic days. We can see by established biblical symbolism that the seven days of creation was an accurate prophecy of how human history would unfold over these seven thousand years. So where are we now?

By using the genealogies in Scripture, we can compute that it has been about six thousand years since Adam was created, or six prophetic days. There is a little ambiguity during the period of the Judges, but according to this timetable we are in or close to the seventh prophetic day, or the Sabbath Day prophetically. Jesus said, **"For the Son of Man is Lord even of the Sabbath" (Matthew 12:8 NKJV).** He was not saying He would be Lord of the last day of each week. Rather, He was speaking of the last day of the prophetic week, the one thousand year day in which He will return to rule over the earth with His faithful ones.

It is clear in the writings of the Early Church Fathers (the direct disciples of the first apostles) that they understood this prophetic week. Their writings are not considered canon

Scripture, but they are well-verified as being authentic. Here is what Barnabas wrote about this prophetic week:

In the beginning of the creation He makes mention of the Sabbath. God made in six days the works of His hands, and He finished them on the seventh day, and He rested the seventh day, and sanctified it. Consider, my children, what that signifies, that He finished them in six days. The meaning of it is this; that in six thousand years the Lord God will bring all things to an end (in the present age). For with Him one day is a thousand years; and He testified, saying, "Behold this day shall be as a thousand years. Therefore, children, in six days, that is, in six thousand years, shall all things be accomplished" (Book of Barnabas 13:2-5).

In these writings of the Early Church Fathers, it is quite clear that the apostles understood the message of I Peter 3:8, which explains why some of them wrote that they were in "the last days." They were saying this in relation to the prophetic week. They knew they were in the final days of this week, or in the last two thousand years before the end of the age.

Children of the Day

We are now coming to the last day of that prophetic week, the Sabbath that Christ will be the Lord over. When explaining how the Lord is going to come suddenly, like a "thief in the night," the Apostle Paul exhorted in I Thessalonians 5:4-5:

But you, brethren, are not in darkness, so that this Day should overtake you as a thief.

You are all sons of light and sons of the day. We are not of the night nor of darkness (NKJV).

The Lord and His apostles put great emphasis on knowing the signs of the times. As this verse states, we should know these signs of the times so well that we are not surprised by the Lord's coming, but rather be expecting it. He said no man would know the day or the hour, but hundreds of biblical prophecies were given to us so we could know the approximate time the King will come, if we are the sons of the light and sons of the day.

Since the 1844 Advent Movement that emphasized the return of Christ, there has been a growing consensus among biblical scholars that we are indeed coming to the end of this age and the return of Christ to rule over the earth. This is sometimes referred to as "the day of the Lord" in Scripture. No biblical term is random, but it is called a "day" for a reason. A major factor in understanding the day of the Lord is when the days were created in Genesis 1. There it is established that the day begins with evening. So we must go through the darkness to get to the dawn. In biblical prophecy this is known as "the great time of trouble."

The coldest, darkest part of the day is just before dawn. This is why some biblical scholars and students of prophecy have been saying that we are already in the day of the Lord. By this they are often referring to the world having already entered the evening part and that it will yet get darker and colder before the dawn. So how close to the dawn are we?

There are many signs given in biblical prophecy to approximate the time of the dawn, but to establish this as it deserves requires much more space than we can give in this work. However, you don't have to be a prophet to see that we are moving fast toward the deepest darkness to come upon the earth. When the Lord's disciples asked Him about the signs of the end of this age, He spoke mostly about the great time of trouble that it would be, but concluded that when we see this we should look up and rejoice because our redemption is near (see Luke 21:28). This darkness will be followed by a brilliant dawn that will cause the greatest rejoicing ever upon the earth.

From this brilliant dawn will come the most glorious age of all, far more wonderful than any religion, utopian philosophy, or dream that even the most illumined have been able to articulate. The Scriptures give general indications of how wonderful it will be, summing it up by simply saying that it will be better than our present minds can conceive.

In short, God so loved the world that He sent His Son to redeem it. It has been redeemed, and next it will be reconciled to Him, and then restored to the Paradise it was originally intended to be. This restoration takes place over what is called in Scripture **"the times of restoration of all things" (see Acts 3:21 NKJV).** It is a period, not just an instant transformation. This period is a thousand years—the thousand year "Day of the Lord."

While we receive the salvation of God the moment we believe in Jesus' atonement on the cross, our restoration from our fallen nature just begins with that. The Lord did not change or mature us in an instant, and neither will it be so for the world. Of course, He has the power to do it instantly if He so chooses, but He wants us to go through this process. It is through the process of restoration that we learn the most about the Lord and His ways. Therefore, this time is not punishment, but a great opportunity to learn of Him and grow closer to Him.

The restoration of the world will be accomplished by the Redeemer, Jesus, and the redeemed from this age are being prepared to rule with Him in the age to come. It is for this reason He will return to set up His kingdom on the earth. He is not coming back just to punish the wicked, but to abolish the wickedness that is destroying the earth and people.

Again, ruling over the earth with Him during this period will be those who followed Him during the present "evil age." These are the ones who have proven their love for Him. They have proven this by standing for Him and doing His will in opposition to the evil spirit of the age. Taking up their crosses daily to follow Him is the cost of their sacrifice. All that this has cost them in this age will be repaid many times over in the age to come.

Transition

Both Jesus and the apostles said this period would come upon the world like birth pangs, or contractions, come upon a woman in childbirth. In natural childbirth the period called "transition" is the most difficult and confusing time before the birth. Likewise, the transition time between the ages will be the challenging period of human history. It will be a time of great confusion and darkness, but not for those who are of the light and who walk in the light. As the world sinks into increasing confusion and disorientation, the Lord will send some of His greatest lights to help her toward the birth.

In natural childbirth, it is during transition that the mother is instructed to have a focal point, which is the father if he is present. She is told that during this period it is crucial she not obey her feelings, but rather his instructions. This is because her feelings will have her doing what is often the opposite of what she should be doing, and his instructions will get her through this time. It is now more crucial than ever that we too have our Focal Point, the Lord, and that we are resolute to follow His instructions, not our feelings.

The Mighty Ones

There is a force more powerful than any human army now gathering to prepare the way for the Lord and His kingdom. There has never been anything like it before, and neither will there be again. You cannot distinguish this army by its uniforms or banners, but it has fortresses in every nation and camps in every city. This force is mostly hidden except to those who are part of it, but soon every soul on earth will hear its trumpets. It is the army of the Lord, and it is here to prepare the way for His coming kingdom.

I was a new believer in 1971 when I first saw this army in visions. Over the years, in little pieces here and there, I have been shown much more about it and those who are called to be a part of it. I have seen their preparation and their positioning. Others have seen them too. These are the mighty ones Enoch prophesied of, a part of which is quoted in the Book of Jude.

Enoch is a special sign to this army. Like Enoch, they will walk with God in the darkest of times. Like Enoch, they will be more at home in heaven than on earth, and they will be witnesses to principalities and powers. They are now beginning to awaken and will soon begin marching to the last battle that is just beginning to unfold.

This army has been seen to some degree by every prophet to walk with the Lord. Prophets see in part, and some prophets have put several parts together for a more complete vision because the time is near. There will be much more synthesis to this vision for this army is now being gathered. To see this army in visions is an honor, but now those who are actually going to be a part of it are here and are coming together. Still, there are many more that do not yet see it clearly, even though they are called to be a part of it. These only know their hearts are burning for something more, and the fire won't go out. They will soon find and become a part of what their hearts are burning for.

The Last Battle

This age will conclude with the ultimate battle between light and darkness. It will be the final confrontation between truth and lies, righteousness and wickedness, justice and injustice. It has been raging in every generation and in every place, but it will soon culminate in the ultimate clash of good and evil. The end of this age is near, and as this last battle is unfolding, everyone on the earth must choose sides. There will be no neutral countries and be no neutral people.

These are the days the prophets of old longed to see, but you have been chosen to live in them. Being alive in these times is one of the greatest honors, but also one of the greatest responsibilities and most difficult tasks. Accomplishing our task begins with understanding the times and knowing our place in them.

Though the emerging generation may have the most difficult task, it will be given the greatest power for accomplishing it. We now have the sure word of prophecy that has unfolded and can be seen and understood from the end looking backward. The unfolding of all that has been predicted and fulfilled up to this time reveals a clear path being laid out. We have a map, a blueprint that the brightest Light of all, Jesus the Christ, has illuminated.

Though the world is sinking into the increasing quagmire of the mystery Babylon (Babylon means "confusion"), those who follow the King will have increasing light and clarity for navigating through these times. There will be a growing distinction between those who walk in the light and those who do not. Those who do not walk in the light will be increasingly confused, and those who do will become clear and confident. The greater the darkness, the more the light will stand out. This is the time when the greatest light, the glory of the Lord, will be revealed, as we are told in Isaiah 60:1-3:

Arise, shine; for your light has come! And the glory of the Lord has risen upon you.

For behold, the darkness shall cover the earth, and deep darkness the peoples; but the Lord will arise over you, and His glory will be seen upon you.

The Nations shall come to your light, and kings to the brightness of your rising (MVB).

So even though it will be getting darker for a time, it is only darker for those who do not walk by the light of the Spirit. Those who have the light in their hearts will not be in confusion or darkness. Therefore, if we are becoming more confused, we have somehow departed from the path. That is a sure sign that we must find where we missed a turn and go back to it and get on the right path. As we are told in Proverbs 4, the path of the righteous always gets brighter.

Never forget that the light will prevail, and the nations are going to come to it. It will be during the time of greatest darkness that the greatest hope the world has ever heard will be broadcast in every place—the good news of the coming kingdom. His kingdom will not only prevail, as Isaiah saw, it will never stop increasing.

CHAPTER TWO

The Gathering

G od has an army that is just beginning to gather. Ultimately, it will be something like an irresistible force and an immovable object. Where it marches, it will conquer. Where it takes a stand, it will not be moved. That this great force is now gathering is one of the great signs that the end of this age is at hand, and the King will soon come to establish His kingdom. We must hear the sound of the trumpet that is now being sounded and respond to it by gathering together with others of like vision and purpose.

Gathering is the crucial first stage that must precede any group becoming an effective force. Because only those who have "ears to hear" can discern the trumpet now being sounded, these gatherings are of those who hear what others cannot, and like Moses, see what others cannot now see—they see **"Him who is invisible" (see Hebrews 11:27 NKJV).** If we see Him, we will follow Him. If we follow Him, we will find the others who are following Him.

Basic Training

After being gathered, or mobilized, every army begins with basic training. This is true of God's army as well. For this reason we can expect a serious emphasis on the basics of the faith to come upon those who are being called. Just as those who are the most successful in every field are those that do the basics best, so it is with Christians. The foundations must be strengthened for anything significant to be built on them. The force to be gathered must be built on the strongest possible foundations.

Our Fortress and Truth is a Person. Our position in Him is as impregnable as our devotion to Him. To be strong in His truth begins with knowing His truth. We must be fortified in His Word, and so we can expect a great love and hunger for His Word to spread among His people. The most basic Christian training of all, the cross, will be our basic devotion again. Then the power won at the cross will be released to those who have taken it up.

Weapons

We are commanded in I Corinthians 14:1 to **"Pursue love, and desire spiritual gifts, but especially that you may prophesy" (NKJV).** The weapons of God's army are not carnal, but spiritual. Love is the most powerful of the divine weapons we have been given. The gifts of the Spirit are one of the main ways that His love is demonstrated. The truth that sets us free that He has given to us in His Word is another. Because our King is the Word, His communication through His prophets has always been a primary way He has related to His people and the world. Prophecy is, therefore, esteemed among the gifts in the New Testament. Few things can impact a person like a word that they know came from God just for them.

We are told in Acts 2:17-18 that when the Lord pours out His Spirit the result is prophetic revelation in dreams, visions, and prophecy. We are also told here that this will be "in the last days." That this is increasing now is another sign that we are approaching the end of this age. These increase at the end of the age because we are going to need this increased guidance.

As remarkable as some of the prophetic gifts are now, we can expect them to increase. We have the testimony of Scripture that what is coming will eclipse anything ever before seen. As we are told in II Corinthians 3, the glory that we are supposed to be seeing in the New Covenant should eclipse even what Moses saw. It will also exceed what was experienced in the first century, which was but the seed of what is now coming to maturity.

This is not to imply that the last-day church will be greater than the first-century church. Just as the rebuilt temple of the Lord was promised a greater glory but was actually an inferior temple, so it may be in these times. However, it is not about the temple. This is about the One whom the temple is for. Would it be better to see a greater temple or a greater glory of the One who is in it?

In 1987, I was shown in *The Vision of the Harvest* that noteworthy miracles would soon become common. From the time I had become a believer in 1971 and when I received that vision in 1987, any miracle or healing was noteworthy. There were a few evangelists and prophets who saw more consistent miracles, but overall they were uncommon. Now it is rare to not hear about what the Scriptures call a **"noteworthy miracle" (see Acts 4:16)** almost every week. Because this has unfolded over several decades, many do not seem to realize how far the body of Christ has come in walking in power. In almost every way the last-day ministry is already beginning to eclipse the power that the first-century church walked in.

Extraordinary healing and miracle ministries emerged during the 1950s, and with the exception of Oral Roberts, seemed to fade away quickly. However, seeds were planted by them, and movements like The Full Gospel Businessmen's Fellowship, The Vineyard, and others emerged, and kept raising the bar as God honored the growing faith of His people. Even so, we are still a long way from walking in all of the authority we are called to have and will need in the days to come. As great as many things now are, who could claim to be walking in a "greater glory" than Moses, as II Corinthians 3 says those in the New Covenant will experience? We must press on. The whole creation is crying out for the full manifestation of the sons of God.

The supernatural acts of God through His people will be some of the weapons of His army. This is because they are demonstrations that He is alive and moving among His people. They are demonstrations of His love, truth, righteousness, peace, and joy. His armory is now stocked with these, and His soldiers are now learning to use them. We will see these becoming more and more powerful.

The Call

As the trumpet call is now being sounded for the mobilizing of God's army, many who have slipped away from their place in the body of Christ are now returning. Independent churches are joining larger movements. We can expect this to continue as more definition, focus, and a greater sense of purpose come upon God's people. Soon we can expect movements to join with other movements and even denominations to join other denominations. With every union, power and authority will be increased, and this is a basic biblical principle.

This great gathering together is from the Lord. Isolation, or loneliness, was the first thing the Lord said was not good. Mankind was created with a need for community. We will have a void in our lives if we are not a vital part of His community. This community of communities is the city that Abraham saw. This is the vision that compelled him to leave everything and wander in unfamiliar places, not knowing where he was going. He may not have known where he was going, but he knew what he was looking for. He wanted to be part of what God was building. He wanted to be part of the city of God. Do we see His city?

The body of Christ, as it was designed to be and will be, is the ultimate community, the great society—a city that will be set on a hill that the whole world will see. There is nothing else like it in all of creation. As it emerges in its ultimate form, every human being will desire to be a part of such communion.

We can never know complete peace or fulfillment until we are in the place we were called to be in the Lord's body. We cannot be properly joined to the Head without also being properly joined to His body. Just as the Apostle John wrote in I John 4:20, **"If someone says, 'I love God,' and hates his brother, he is a liar; for the one who does not love his brother whom he has seen, how can he love God whom he has not seen?" (NKJV)**

Growing Pains

To be a part of His body is not easy during its formative, maturing stages. It is not easy then, but that is when we can derive the most benefit from the experience. This is when we have the greatest opportunity to grow in love and the fruit of the Spirit. We need the frustrations and irritations that naturally occur in a true community of believers to be changed so that we can fit into our place. Without this there is a serious limit on our spiritual maturity.

We may want the church to be mature and get over all of its problems before we join it, but then we would miss out on what we need to get over our own problems, the chance for our own growth. If we are waiting for the church to mature before we join it, by the time it gets to the place where it would be acceptable to us, it will be so far advanced compared to us that we will not likely catch up.

A vital, local church life is essential for true spiritual maturity. This is where the army of God is mobilizing. If we are not a part of a body of believers, we can grow in knowledge, we can still have spiritual experiences, and even operate in the gifts of the Spirit with increasing power, but we will be limited in our true maturity in Christ. This will severely limit the ultimate authority with which we can be trusted. In the times to come, even survival itself will be dependent upon our being in our place in the body of Christ, just as we are warned in I Corinthians 11:23-29:

> **For I received from the Lord that which I also delivered to you: that the Lord Jesus in the night in which He was betrayed took bread;**
> **and when He had given thanks, He broke it, and said, "Take, eat; this is My body which is broken for you; do this in remembrance of Me."**
> **In the same manner He also took the cup after supper, saying, "This cup is the new covenant in My blood. This do, as often as you drink it, in remembrance of Me."**
> **For as often as you eat this bread and drink the cup, you proclaim the Lord's death until He comes.**
> **Therefore whoever eats the bread or drinks the cup of the Lord in an unworthy manner shall be guilty of the body and the blood of the Lord.**
> **But let a man examine himself, and so let him eat of the bread and drink of the cup.**
> **For he who eats and drinks in an unworthy manner eats and drinks judgment to himself, not discerning the Lord's body (NKJV).**

The way we partake of communion in an unworthy manner is to partake of the ritual without having the reality that it represents in our lives. What this ritual represents is true communion, or common-union. Communion is not something we take occasionally, but something we must have in our lives. One of the greatest stumbling blocks to Christians walking in what they are called to walk in has been the tendency to substitute rituals for the realities they represent. By this, one drinks **"judgment to himself, not discerning the Lord's body" (see I Corinthians 11:29 NKJV).** To "judge the body rightly" is to discern the body, our part in it, and to get there. That is true communion, or common-union.

If you were to cut off any part of the body, it would get weak and sick, rapidly dying if it were not quickly and properly reattached. This too is true of Christians when they leave the body. They may temporarily feel relief when they leave because they are relieved of certain pressures and trials. However, those are the pressures and trials intended to fashion them into a vessel they are called to be in the King's service.

Life or Death

In the times we are entering, it will become increasingly costly not to be in our place in the Lord's body. Then it will become a matter of life and death. There is no safer place to be on this earth than in the Lord's will. The most basic aspect of being in His will is fitting together rightly with the rest of His body.

On the other hand, for those who are in His will, or their place in His body, there will be ever-increasing peace, joy, and fulfillment as we are doing what we are called to do. With the present structure of the church, we may think this is extremely hard to do, but the structure of the church will soon change. This change will come from those who are resolutely pursuing their purpose in His body and will not be denied it.

The bride of Christ will become all she is called to be. She will be like nothing the earth has ever before seen. Even the first-century church was but a seed of what the church will be at the harvest, the end of the age, when all things come to their ultimate conclusion.

Both the light and darkness are coming to full maturity in these times, and so evil is also mobilizing for the last battle. This is to be expected. As the Lord explained in the Parable of the Wheat and Tares, the tares must be bundled together and taken out before the wheat is harvested. This is why we are now seeing those who are evil being gathered into their special interests as well.

Enlisting

Even if you are called to be a part of this great force now gathering, you do not have to respond to the call. It is your choice. The army of the Lord is a volunteer army. As Psalm 110:3 states, His people will volunteer freely in the day of His power. If you are called to be a part of this, it is time to find your place. If you do not want it, then He will give your commission to someone who will value it. As we see in Scripture, the firstborn, or first chosen, often reject their calling. However, there will be those who will esteem His calling as the greatest opportunity one can have in this life, as it is, and they will do anything it takes to be a part of His purpose.

How will we know our place if we are not yet in it? We must use the "key to the kingdom." The key to the kingdom is what we use to unlock the door to the kingdom. This key is to seek the kingdom first in everything we do. Only the key to the kingdom can unlock the way for us.

When we are in our place, we will know it. If we are questioning whether we are in the right place or not, we can be pretty sure we are not. If this is the case, we must go back and look at the major decisions we have made in our life and consider if we may have made them from any other motive than seeking His will.

Ask the Lord to help you get in your place. If we are serious about this, He will help us. As we are told in Romans 12, if we have had our minds renewed, which is the result of following Him as we are called, we can **"prove what is that good and acceptable and perfect will of God" (see Romans 12:2 NKJV).** Those who are walking in His will can "prove" that they are in His will. We are called to live by that confidence. However, to do this, we must respond to His call and then stay resolutely focused on doing His will.

I talk to many Christians who do not feel there is a church near them they fit into. This is because there isn't. They do not fit into a body near them because they are in the wrong place. They are in the wrong place because they made the decision about where they would live based on the best job opportunity, geography they liked, or even to be close to friends or relatives, instead of making this decision based on where the Lord wanted them—discerned by seeking first His kingdom.

Of course, many Christians fire off a prayer to heaven for guidance and consider that all they need to do to seek His will.

Then they continue doing what they want to do. The kingdom of God is much more serious business. As soldiers of Christ, we must wait for orders if we do not have them. It can be a hard way to live at times, but it's much harder not to live this way.

If we have lived according to our own will and wisdom until now, it can change if we are willing to change. We can be a part of the greatest force for good if we resolve to be the soldiers we are called to be. It does not matter how many mistakes we have made, or how many years we have wasted. It doesn't matter how old or young we are, we can still be a part.

If we would make all of our major decisions based on seeking the kingdom and His righteousness first, then He promises that everything else will be added to us. However, if we do not seek the kingdom first, then we can likely count on there being constant discord and frustration in our lives. We can be in the wrong place and have a great job, make a lot of money, and accumulate many possessions, while being empty and without peace, not to mention losing our loved ones.

Even if we have been out of the will of God for a long time, we can take the key to the kingdom right now, open the door to the kingdom, and enter it. It may mean leaving where you are, changing jobs, even for a lower salary and benefits, but there is no greater benefit than being in God's will. He promises to add everything else we need if we will seek His kingdom first. The important thing, the critical thing, is that we are in His will.

CHAPTER THREE

Going Deeper

I n Scripture there are two curses that come upon nations that turn from God: 1) to have capricious, arrogant, and unrighteous leaders, and 2) prophets that speak words to please the people rather than the true words from God. Could there be a more accurate description of the world's most powerful leaders in virtually every field, or the typical message coming from the church? In II Timothy 4:3-5 we are given a sober warning:

For the time will come when they will not endure sound doctrine, but according to their own desires, because they have itching ears, they will heap up for themselves teachers;

and they will turn their ears away from the truth, and be turned aside to fables.

But you be watchful in all things, endure afflictions, do the work of an evangelist, fulfill your ministry (NKJV).

When was the last time you heard a sermon calling you to endure hardship? When was the last time you heard a sermon on sin or repentance? How about taking up our crosses, or loving not our lives even to death? You will not hear them because they are hard for people to hear, and there is a greater emphasis in much of the church on what will attract people rather than speaking the truth. For this reason much of the body of Christ in the West is either asleep or lukewarm. Studies have revealed that there is almost no discernable difference between Christians and unbelievers in basic morality and integrity. It could be that the church in the West is the weakest it has ever been.

Having been raised in such Christian weakness is why so many will fall away, and even turn against their brothers and sisters in Christ, as is predicted in the Scriptures about the end of the age. Some will awaken, and some will be baptized with the fire of the Holy Spirit. Never give up on anyone who still calls on the name of Jesus. However, there is another fellowship, and it is growing, though it will always be relatively small. It is the fellowship of the true messengers that are also called "flames of fire" (see Hebrews 1:7).

Even though it may be few that can now hear the call to endure hardship, those few will be enough. They are of a different spirit. These can embrace sound doctrine, and as Proverbs says about the truly wise, they will love reproof and correction. They will also remain vigilant and sober in spirit, keeping their vessels always full of the oil of the Holy Spirit. They will endure hardship and will not run from their trials. Those who have remained resolute in the midst of growing deception and the compromising spirit of the times will become some of the most remarkable leaders of all time.

There are a number of things that we can expect to separate the wheat from the tares. This separation is going on presently in the body of Christ, and we know it will increase. Those who will only listen to what they want to hear are being given over to immature, unrighteous leadership. The Christians who are in this weak, vulnerable, delusional condition can change, but if they do not change soon the consequences will be most severe. Those whose hearts are given over to the comforts of this present world will suffer the fate of this present world.

Those who can hear the truth, who are willing to now endure hardship for their training when they could take the easy route like most others, will become righteous leaders of the future. The future will belong to them.

The Warriors

This is not to imply that all we should talk about are the hard times to come, but the breakdown comes with those who cannot hear about them at all. Most of what Jesus and the apostles spoke about concerning the end was the troubles, but we must walk in the faith that sees that there is an opportunity to see the glory and victory of the Lord, even in the most difficult times. True warriors do not run from the sound of battle, but to it. They know there cannot be a victory without a battle.

The Scriptures verify that mature leaders are those who have been through the fire. These trials can even be created from their own mistakes and failures, but true leaders do not quit when they make mistakes and do not stay down when they fall. If we want leaders who have not made mistakes, we should consider how Captain Smith was chosen to skipper the Titanic because he had never had an accident at sea. How did that work out?

One cause for so many following immature or unrighteous leaders is found in II Corinthians 11:19-20:

For you put up with fools gladly, since you yourselves are wise!
For you put up with it if one brings you into bondage, if one devours you, if one takes from you, if one exalts himself, if one strikes you on the face (NKJV).

It is remarkable how many Christians who gravitate to the easiest messages and lowest levels of commitment so easily follow those who minister in a controlling spirit rather than the Holy Spirit. Carnal people will follow carnal authority and reject true spiritual authority. Just as many people are conditioned to respond to the hype of television commercials and can hardly pay attention to one that is done with class and dignity, many Christians respond more quickly to hype than to the anointing, sometimes confusing the two. Our King has the greatest class and dignity, and His true followers can discern the imposters.

Wisdom

Truth is sometimes negative in the sense that it points to what is wrong when that is needed. The most important truth for us at a given time can be correction. Therefore, the right response to truth is not always excitement, but is sometimes remorse. Again, as repeated often in Proverbs, the wise love reproof, and those who harden themselves to reproof will go on to destruction.

John the Baptist preached repentance to prepare the way for the Lord's first coming, and repentance must be preached to prepare for His second coming. The Holy Spirit is about to come in His nature as the One who convicts of sin. If that does not make us feel good, it is because it is not supposed to. It is supposed to make us remorseful enough to repent of our sin and return to the Lord. If we are not willing to be convicted of our sin, or our irrational and continuing immaturity, we will miss the greatest move of God of all time, and very well could end up on the wrong side at the end.

Weak, immature Christians gravitate to preachers who tell them what they want to hear, not what they need to hear. The greatest preachers and teachers in history, who accomplished the most for the gospel and the kingdom of God, were those who brought conviction and repentance, yet also concluded with the remedy—the cross of Jesus Christ. The strongest Christians have always been those who embraced the cross and learned to take up the cross every day.

Even though the Western church may now be the weakest it has ever been, there is still some strength in it. There is still hope that she will wake up and repent of what has led her to this state. We must never give up hope that the weaknesses cannot only be corrected, but can be transformed into an even greater strength. There is no power like the power of redemption that works through the cross.

We can be sure that the cross will become the central theme of Christianity again. The way of the cross will be the way of life for all who go on to maturity. Those who do not embrace it will fall away from the faith in the coming times because the way of the cross is the only path through them. Some who fall away may continue to lead big churches or big movements, but they will be the blind leading the blind. They will not get out of the ditch they have fallen into if they do not learn to repent.

The army of God that is gathering will march under the banner of the cross. It is the army of the cross. There is no other way to true discipleship in Christ, and the way of the cross is the path of life. His soldiers live the cross, taking it up daily, and thereby prove to be the Lord's true disciples. There are other things that define His disciples, such as their love, but the ultimate demonstration of God's love was the cross. The true love for God and others is demonstrated by those who take up their crosses to follow Him.

God's army may not be large, but there has never been one more powerful. These will refuse to retreat before the enemies of the cross, and their faithfulness even to death is more powerful than death. They will not be afraid to die because they will have already died to this world, and they live to do all things for the sake of His gospel. Are we one of these?

Power

No bomb ever made is as powerful as what is contained in a single believer who has the Spirit of God living in them. Until now we have only seen occasional glimpses of this power being demonstrated through a few. What is coming will be the true "greatest show on earth." There has never been anything like it, nor will there be anything like it again. These are the times when even greater things than Jesus did will be done in His name, just as He promised.

The most basic training in the use of God's power is to understand the basic principle of walking in His supernatural power. This is stated in I Corinthians 1:18: **"For the word of the cross is foolishness to those who are perishing, but to us who are being saved it is the power of God."**

So **"the word of the cross . . . is the power of God" (see I Corinthians 1:18).** This is hard for all who have not had their minds transformed. Until we see with spiritual eyes, it does not make sense that if we lose our lives we find them. The cross is the most powerful force that has ever been on the earth. It even has the power over death. It is the power of a life fully surrendered to God and His will that enables Him to fully reveal Himself through them.

Healing Bombs

Jesus taught the truth that sets men free. He delivered people from what was oppressing them and healed their bodies from what was afflicting them. That is the power of the gathering army of God. They do not conquer, but set captives free. They do not wound, but heal. They do not kill, but give life.

God's love is the foundation of true spiritual authority. It was when Jesus felt compassion for the sheep without a shepherd that He became their Shepherd. When He felt compassion for those who walked in darkness, He became their Teacher. It is compassion that leads us to His purpose. This is also why we are commanded to love our enemies. If we will love them, we will be able to help set them free, leading them to salvation, the greatest victory of all over our enemies.

If you feel compassion in your heart for a people group, a nation, or even something more general such as music or a field in science, it could be leading you to your calling. This is often how He begins to release His authority through us. His authority is for redemption, reconciliation, and restoration, and it is always founded upon love because God is love.

When we have this compassion for something that seems unnatural, it could be because it is supernatural. When it is for something as general as a supernatural love for music, it is more than just loving to listen to it or playing it, but should include a concern for its purity and health. Maybe you are called to help bring healing to music, to give it direction and purpose that would keep it pure. But how could you practically do this?

This could come by a proclamation of truth or a prophetic word with the power of God behind it. It could come by producing music that so raises the bar that others who have musical gifts are convicted if they fall short of this standard. When music has His anointing, being used as God intended, it first captures people's attention and then their hearts. This could lead to a demonstration of music from heaven the way God originally designed music. When this happens, all other music will start to seem crude, and even perverted, in comparison.

At times we have had glimpses of this at MorningStar University's School of Worship. When there is a gathering of students with a heart for this, it has created something like a spiritual critical mass. This can set off a spiritual nuclear explosion. This kind of explosion does not blow things apart, but rather gathers and melds hearts together. Some of our students who experienced this have gone on to become successful worship leaders and songwriters. It was that experience in the critical mass that ignited what was being released through them to others.

This has also happened from time to time with those who have prophetic gifts. As those with these gifts bond, a power is released that is much greater. This seems to happen when those who are gathering begin to prefer one another, which is one way that we go to the cross.

Seeing the Pearl

For years both the immature prophetic ministries and some of the spiritually immature musicians were costly to have around. We had to love both of these through some trying times when we wondered if it would be worth it. Until that critical mass happened, it took a lot of faith to endure the challenges. Yet, now it was worth it many times over. We would have never received the treasure if we had not had the faith and patience that is required to receive the promises of God.

Growing our faith is more valuable than gold, as we are told in I Peter 1:7. God will seldom miss an opportunity to grow our faith, which means putting us in a place where we are going to need a lot more of it. The ultimate demonstration of faith could be patience.

Everyone wants the mature fruit, but not many are willing to do what it takes to plant a tree and cultivate it until it has matured and can bear fruit. The price of bearing spiritual fruit is to take up our crosses daily, not occasionally. We must live not seeking our own will, but His. It is a life that is not self-seeking, but self-sacrificing. Even so, just one moment of the glory and anointing of God that we experience is worth any sacrifice many times over.

It is a basic spiritual principle that between the place where we receive the promise of God and the Promised Land, or the fulfillment of the promises, there will be a wilderness that is the opposite of what we have been promised. We must learn to endure the hard, dry times in order to get to the land flowing with milk and honey. Even so, in the wilderness we will experience great things, and that is where the dwelling place of God was built in the midst of His people. Don't waste your trials. It will be hard at times, but it will always be worth it.

It is a sound principle that anything that happens too fast or too easily is usually insignificant. If you develop faster spiritually, it will probably require much more intense training. A great mobilization is taking place, and things are happening faster, but it will always take faith and patience to inherit the promises. Those who do not have these will be weeded out by the trials ahead. Those who have faith and patience will gain more of each through the trials. This is so that they can be trusted with the unprecedented power that must be released at the end of this age.

CHAPTER FOUR

A Bride in Boots

How will the army of God be like earthly armies? How will it be different? These are important questions to answer in the beginning because they have everything to do with how the army is formed. Here are a few of the basics:

Ways that God's army will be like a human army:

1) It will be composed of people mobilized and trained for the purpose of defeating an enemy.

2) Its soldiers will be trained to specialize in the use of different weapons.

3) It will have military discipline and focus.

4) It will have clear objectives, strategies, and tactics.

5) Like every army, there will be two basic parts—those

39

who engage the enemy and those devoted to the support and supply of those on the front lines.

Ways that God's army will not be like a human army:

1) It will fight to give life, not take it.

2) It will fight to free people, not conquer them.

3) Its victory is not the destruction of those controlled by the enemy, but rather the tearing down of strongholds that are keeping them in bondage so as to set them free.

4) Its weapons are not carnal, but spiritual.

5) The battles, objectives, strategies, and tactics will be spiritual, not physical.

The above is corroborated in a number of Scriptures, but we will review just a few, beginning with II Corinthians 10:3-6:

For though we walk in the flesh, we do not war according to the flesh.

For the weapons of our warfare are not carnal but mighty in God for pulling down strongholds,

casting down arguments and every high thing that exalts itself against the knowledge of God, bringing every thought into captivity to the obedience of Christ,

and being ready to punish all disobedience when your obedience is fulfilled (NKJV).

To understand this spiritual army we must learn the ways of the Spirit. Some of these ways are different from the ways we have learned in the natural. The natural realm is called a shadow of the spiritual realm. What we think of as real has far less substance than the spiritual realm, just as a shadow is but a reflection of what it is reflecting.

Likewise, many natural laws are a reflection of spiritual laws, but not all. There is spiritual communication, or "spiritual words," of such greater substance than any human language that human languages are like a shadow compared to them. These can only be comprehended with a spiritual mind.

For this reason, to be a part of this spiritual army of God, we must have our minds renewed in order to **"prove what is that good and acceptable and perfect will of God" (see Romans 12:2 NKJV).** We might say this is required so we can get clear orders or instructions. There are basic ways we must learn to think differently, and they are better, more accurate, and truthful ways to think.

When we begin to see into the spiritual realm, the whole natural realm begins to seem small, even insignificant, and in some ways, even a shackle to our souls. However, we must keep in mind that God gave infinite value to this natural realm by coming into it, living as a man, making atonement for the whole world (not just man), and determining that He would dwell on the earth with man.

The natural realm has great value, yet it is only when it is reconnected to the spiritual realm and to the Lord, who is Spirit, that it can be what it was created to be. The **"new creation" (see II Corinthians 5:17)**, those who are born again by the Spirit, are called to be the bridge between the spiritual and natural realms, for they live in both.

For this reason, our purpose is to make heaven our home even more than the earth, bringing heaven to the earth. When His kingdom comes, His will is done on earth as it is in heaven. To prepare the way for His kingdom we must do His will now. Therefore, our goal is not to just become spiritual, but so spiritual that we are a practical help to prepare the earth for His coming.

Combat Compassion

As General Douglas MacArthur said, "It is fatal to enter any war without the will to win it." It is likewise dangerous to enter any type of combat without the resolve to win. We can only know if we have won when we have clear objectives. It was said of Jesus that He came **"to destroy the works of the devil" (see I John 3:8 NKJV).** In John 17:18, Jesus said that as He had been sent into the world, so is He sending us. For this reason our ultimate purpose is to destroy the works of the enemy and to see his bondage over mankind entirely broken so that man can be fully restored to God.

During conflict even a moment's hesitancy when opportunity presents itself can turn a victory into a defeat. Therefore, we must be clear about our objectives, and our resolve must be steadfast. Because this last-day army of God is different from any other army and our victory looks different, this must be clearly defined before we engage the enemy.

He Created Us Male and Female

The church is called to be both the bride of Christ and an army of God. This is a seeming conflict of nature that is hard for many to understand, much less embrace. The bride is feminine, and the martial nature of an army is basically masculine. However, if men must be a part of the bride of Christ, then women can be in the army of God. In fact, women can be some of the greatest spiritual warriors, but the point is we all learn to walk in both of these natures to a degree.

This does not mean men are to become more feminine and women more masculine. What it does mean is that men are called to be devoted lovers of God and worshippers, and women must become warriors. We are all called to be both.

This being said, we must also keep in mind that one basic strategy of the devil is to blur the distinctions God created, such as those between men and women. One of his primary goals at the end is to make women into men and men into women. Great female warriors can still be feminine, and great worshippers can be masculine.

It is noteworthy that the church is presently led mostly by men, but its nature is mostly feminine. For this reason, men can have a difficult time relating to present church life and structure. This is why more than 70% of the church is composed of women, and many of the men who are in the church today are not really connected in their hearts. It is not just that women tend to be more spiritual than men, though this may be the case, but most men do not relate to the church in its present form. They are bored with it, or feel out of place. As the church takes on more of the martial nature it is called to have, we will see men flocking back to the church wanting to be a part of it.

As the church develops more of its martial nature, the feminine nature will also grow, keeping the church balanced as it prepares to be the bride of Christ. Again, as King David was one of the greatest warriors in Scripture and also one of the greatest worshippers, the church must grow up in both of these.

His Martial Nature

For many years I have studied the military and military strategies. I have done this because I was shown that the end-time body of Christ would become an army. God uses the title "Lord of hosts" or "Lord of armies" ten times more than all His other titles combined. He is a martial God. We must understand this aspect of His nature and how His people are going to conform to it. To do this, we must understand the many ways in which human martial demeanor is not the same as God's martial demeanor. As we read in Isaiah 55:8-9:

"For My thoughts are not your thoughts, nor are your ways My ways," says the Lord.
"For as the heavens are higher than the earth, so are My ways higher than your ways, and My thoughts than your thoughts" (NKJV).

God's martial nature is much higher than man's martial nature. We need to understand how. We have covered some of the basics of the similarities and differences in strategy and character between human armies and God's army, which can be hard to fully grasp. When we do, and they begin to fit together, our effectiveness will increase. For this reason, we will continue to dig deeper into these similarities and differences.

Fighting for Life

The Lord said that He came to give us abundant life. That does not necessarily mean it will all be good, but that there will be a lot of it! Nothing that can be experienced in this life is more exciting than the true Christian life. There is also nothing more boring than religion. If we are trapped in a dull spiritual life, then we are not on the path of life Jesus came to lead us on. A basic objective is to get on the path of life and stay on it.

One of the primary draws in military recruitment is that young men tend to think of war as an adventure. This can be true to a degree, as there are few things more exciting than marching off to different places and combat. Yet when real conflict is experienced, the adventure part usually turns into the worst kind of hell. Not so in God's army. The adventure is real, and combat in His army is one of the most exhilarating things we can ever be a part of. When the true adventure of Christianity is recovered by the body of Christ, the youth will flock to it, as the biblical prophecies declared.

Every Christian denomination began as a movement. When a movement stops moving it becomes an institution. Many of these have done much good and continue to do good. Many have been true salt and light, yet we have not been called to an institution but to the greatest adventure one can experience in this life—the path of life. It is not all about adventure, but this is one of its great benefits. It is a primary thing giving Christianity its great vitality, inspiring those on the path to constant awe and wonder at the great things God is doing through them.

I have never met anyone who has a goal of living an insignificant or boring life. When the Lord made man, He commanded the man to **"be fruitful and multiply" (see Genesis 1:22).** So it is in our nature that we do not just want to have fruit, but a lot of it. It is deep within the nature of every human being to accomplish, and to accomplish something significant. We are all here to leave a trail of great accomplishments. We are called to fulfill the Lord's command to bear fruit, and fruit that remains.

If your life, and especially your church life, is boring, you are not in the right place. There is nothing more interesting than God, and the closer we get to Him and follow Him, the more exciting our lives will be. There is no greater adventure than the true Christian life, but there is also no life more difficult. We are not called to an easy life, but we are called to a life of significance. Wimps do not make good Christians. God is mobilizing an army of resolute, fearless warriors, and they are being trained for conflict. It will be hard, but it will be worth it. If we follow Him and not just a religion, it will not be boring.

CHAPTER FIVE

Strategy

There is a power in concentration. For example, light that is highly focused, such as a laser, can cut through even dense physical matter. Spiritually, the same can be said of truth. Now we must apply this to the spiritual conflict that is unfolding in the world.

Concentration of Forces

The military strategy called "concentration of forces" has been the most successful of all strategies in the great battles of history. It can also be a key to a successful life. One example is how most of us still have a couple of hundred things wrong with us. It is the devil's strategy to get us to try to fix all of them at the same time. He knows this will so disperse our energy that it cannot be done and will lead frustration, weariness, and ultimately, defeat. As Daniel 7:25 reveals, a basic strategy of the devil is to wear out the saints. Since we are zealous for the Lord, and we want to correct our problems for Him and our loved ones, most Christians fall to this ploy. Those who do not wise up to this often backslide thinking it is just not possible for them to live the Christian life.

The Lord wants to help us, and He sent the Helper. He begins by convicting us of our sin. Then He leads us to the truth that will set us free. The Holy Spirit's strategy is to do this in the most effective way, which is to concentrate on one thing at a time. He knows that if we have a breakthrough in just one area it will lead to victory in many areas.

The Apostle Paul wrote in Philippians 3:13, **"one thing I do."** If we were to concentrate on a breakthrough in just one area we would likely see a quick victory. This is the concentration of forces strategy in action. As once stated by a Civil War general, his victory was achieved by "getting there first with the most."

We will make much faster progress in overcoming our strongholds and problems by concentrating on just one at a time. This does not mean that you don't deal with or completely overlook the other issues while you focus on one. In a real battle, you would leave enough forces to hold the enemy in place while you are concentrating in one place for the main attack. So we can use some effort to keep our other issues in check while our main focus is on one area. Ultimately, however, we do not want to let other issues detract from our main focus more than is necessary until we have victory in that area.

Breakthrough Strategy

Using the concentration of forces, our purpose is to create a breakthrough. Once a breakthrough in the lines is accomplished the enemy must retreat to keep opposing forces from getting into its rear area, destroying their supplies, and potentially surrounding its frontline troops. However, we must have a strategy for after the breakthrough, or we can lose all of the ground gained, or worse, open ourselves up to a successful counter-attack by the enemy.

Many defeats have followed great victories in military history because there was a breakdown in the focus and discipline after the breakthrough. Often the troops breaking through the enemy lines would start to plunder the enemy's camp instead of continuing to pursue the enemy. This enabled the enemy to regroup and counterattack a force now in disarray. To prevent this we need to have an immediate follow-up strategy for the breakthrough that goes right to the next objective, and most importantly, keeps the forces in martial array.

A Strategy for Defeat

In contrast to the concentration of forces, the strategy that has probably been the least successful in military history has been fighting on too many fronts. This flawed strategy has been implemented by the church for much of its history and is a major reason why there has been so much defeat. Albert Einstein's definition of insanity, "doing the same things over and over again and expecting different results," has too often applied here.

Consider all of the fronts that the church is fighting on now. They may all be worthy causes, but there is little or no progress in any of them because we have spread our forces so thin. What would happen if we started to concentrate on just one or two areas? We would see real victories, with big and continuous advances.

Right now the church is so divided it is hard to imagine the kind of unity it would require to implement a church-wide strategy, but the foundation of this unity is now being laid. Our Leader will pull this off in due time. Until there is the kind of unity required for victory, almost any level of concentration we can begin to implement can have good results.

Again, this does not mean we do not consider that the enemy is attacking on more than one front. Sometimes you do have to fight more than one battle at a time. However, there are some battles we should be strategically ignoring so we can concentrate on an area where a breakthrough can be achieved. One major victory can so encourage the soldiers that they will push harder. It would also likely mobilize many for the upcoming battles, leading to more victories.

The Initiative

When we start moving from triumph to triumph the way we should be, we will not be continually reacting to the enemy. We will be the ones setting the agenda with our attacks on his strongholds. Another basic military strategy is to "seize the initiative." Every general knows there cannot be an ultimate victory until their side is setting the agenda, forcing the enemy to react to their moves. It is crucial for a force to not lose the initiative, and if they do so, they must recover the initiative as soon as possible. Control of the initiative is critical for success.

When we get to the place where we are not just reacting to what the enemy is throwing at us, but rather are the ones taking the initiative in the battle, the end will be near and the victory of light over darkness assured. It is encouraging that many are now rising up in the body of Christ with the resolve to retreat no further. That is an important start, but to actually bring down enemy strongholds, we must seize and hold the initiative.

Keeping Victories

If we are resolved to take back the lost territory we need greater goals. We cannot slow down or stop because we have regained some ground. Christianity currently is making huge gains around the world, far more than any other religion. But in Christianity's greatest haven, the West, we may have lost more ground in the last fifty years than in the previous five hundred. We cannot give up any more ground, and we must retake what has been lost. When this begins to happen, we must learn to solidify the gains, occupying the land taken while continuing to advance.

As we are told in Psalm 24:1, **"The earth is the Lord's, and all its fullness, the world, and those who dwell in it."** The Lord's kingdom is going to come to the earth, and His will is going to be done on the earth just as it is in heaven. We must keep in mind that our ultimate goal is big, but we must also be practical and able to concentrate on the next step. It is time to see victories. When the church starts experiencing breakthroughs, Christians everywhere will gather in unity to fight the good fight of faith.

At times the church has made effective use of the concentration of forces strategy, resulting in breakthroughs. Yet ultimately, the ground was lost because there was no plan to hold the ground. We saw this exemplified in the natural when the Coalition Forces defeated Saddam Hussein in the second Gulf War. The Coalition destroyed Saddam's forces and took the entire nation of Iraq. The world was relieved, but few foresaw that because they did not have a clear occupation plan the biggest battle of all would come in trying to hold their gains. A devastating insurgent war followed, which ultimately opened the door for ISIS to capture much of the country. Now Iraq is, to a large extent, occupied by a force worse than Saddam Hussein.

The Lord warned that when a demon is cast out of a person and is allowed back in, the latter state is worse than the former. The same is true of spiritual ground taken in nations. When the enemy retakes territory he brings reinforcements. It is always right to resist evil, but we need to think beyond just fighting to winning battles. When the U.S. went into Vietnam without a clear strategy for victory it was an effort doomed from the beginning. Without a resolve to win we can end up in worse shape than when we started in a conflict. We need a strategy for victory, but also one for occupying the ground taken or our victories will lead to even worse defeats.

Counting the Cost

It is no small matter to mobilize people for a campaign. Unless it is a forced campaign by a government that can institute a draft, the people will only respond to a call they believe in. Even if they respond out of conviction, they will quickly leave if they do not believe in the leadership. Once people are gathered they must stay encouraged, which means "to have courage." A major basis for courage comes from believing you will win. Any army will lose courage after it has either suffered repeated defeat or a workable strategy for ultimate victory is not communicated.

That being said, defeat happens. In Scripture we see that even some of the greatest victories of God's people were preceded by defeats. The Lord showed them why they had been defeated, and then the people rose up again and kept fighting. Defeats can be stepping stones to an ultimate victory if we learn from them. As former college football Coach Mike Gottfried once told me, "There are games you win, and games you learn."

For every victory he experienced, General George Washington had many defeats. Even so, his leaders and his army learned from each setback. With each loss they got better at standing up to the well-trained and disciplined British forces. Even in defeat, if a force feels they are getting better and stronger it will be a basis for courage.

That being said, ultimately we need victories to keep going. General Washington wisely picked a few small battles. Even though they were not really strategic he knew he could win them, and he knew they would encourage his army. The courage these small battles brought to Washington's troops may have been more important than some of the much bigger, more strategic battles. The point is that sometimes we need to pick smaller battles that we know we can win, even though they are not as glamorous or seemingly as important as others.

The Playbook

In recent times, the body of Christ in America has not had many big victories. Much of it in the West is, at this writing, in automatic retreat mode. Much of the Western church has an eschatology (study of biblical prophecies about the end of the age) that is basically just getting ready to abandon ship. However, an encouraging trend is that much of the church is beginning to embrace a more victorious eschatology. The focus is growing on the end of the age being the harvest rather than just the tribulation.

Theology is important. Wrong teachings can have a tragic impact. Over the last two centuries, eschatology has become a major focus for what I call the advancing church, which is where almost 90% of church growth is currently. There is an increasing sense that we are coming to a great culmination of the age. Different eschatological teachings have emerged, and we can now judge them by their fruit, as we should. This is leading to a lot of questioning, which is important and good when done in the right spirit.

I have studied every major eschatological position to at least some degree, discovering some merit and good fruit in most of them. However, some positions have resulted in Christians disconnecting from the world to such a degree that they have lost the power to be the salt and light. This allows them to wrongly justify setbacks as being the cross they are called to bear.

There are numerous ways that the different eschatological teachings conflict with each other, but some even have basic conflicts with themselves. That does not concern me as much as when some of the basic tenants of a particular view conflict with Scripture. This is usually the result of making bold, overly specific conclusions about something the Scriptures are ambiguous about, and then neglecting the other biblical teachings that might give us a different perspective. This is why mature debate is both healthy and necessary in such matters.

The Root of Heresy

Almost every heresy is the result of people trying to carry what God has revealed in part to its seemingly logical conclusion. Then, many start using adherence to their revelation as a litmus test for the "faithful." When this happens, we would do well to get far from that group. Such are almost impossible to mobilize with the rest of the body of Christ, and they are headed for increasing deception.

I am addressing this because it is hard to teach about being prepared for the times without addressing eschatology that has within it the seeds of defeat instead of victory. As we read in Isaiah 60, the battle between light and darkness is won by the light, not the darkness. Ultimately the nations are going to come to the light. That which the Scriptures are clear about will ultimately be embraced by all who are walking in the light.

Most of the disunity in the body of Christ is based on issues that are unclear in the Scriptures. Genuine lovers of truth will not usually get caught up in the petty issues that cause division. We need to hold lightly to theories and be tolerant of others who disagree with us about them. Those who have a strong basis for their position don't have to be reactionary. Those who are overly reactionary with those who disagree with them are usually doing this because of the weakness of their position or personal insecurities.

Walking in the light is staying close to the Lord. Doctrines are important, but walking in truth is more than just following a creed. If we are going to unite for the battle we need to begin with what we can agree on. One point of agreement should be the Lord's own statement in Matthew 24:14: **"And this gospel of the kingdom will be preached in all the world as a witness to all the nations, and then the end will come"** (NKJV).

The Goal

More Christians are beginning to understand that the gospel of the kingdom is not the same as the gospel of salvation. The gospel of our salvation is a foundational pillar of the gospel of the kingdom, but it is far from the complete gospel of the kingdom. The gospel of the kingdom is not about our personal salvation as much as it is about the world's salvation. The King is returning to set up His kingdom on earth, with His will being done on the earth as it is in heaven (see Matthew 6:10).

As the Lord told Nicodemus, we must be born again before we can see the kingdom (see John 3:3). That being understood, a basic characteristic of God's army is that it is not the army of an earthly kingdom. Rather, it is an army of the kingdom of God. To be a part of it, we must meet the King, see the kingdom, and be willing to lay down our lives to prepare the way for the Lord.

This is not to imply that Christians should not be involved in their nation's politics or the affairs of this world. In some cases, they should mobilize to aid in the cause. However, there is an army being gathered that cannot be distracted from its purpose to preach the gospel of the kingdom to prepare the way for the Lord. The Lord is not coming as a Republican or a Democrat, a liberal or a conservative, a socialist or a capitalist. He is not coming to take sides. He is coming to take over.

The basis of every kingdom is that the king's authority is recognized. Obedience to King Jesus is the most basic principle of living in His kingdom and preaching the gospel of the kingdom. Knowing His voice and obeying it are basic to those who would mobilize as part of God's army.

Hearing

In basic training, the first thing you are taught is to march in step with others. This is true whether you are in the Army, Navy, Marines, or Air Force. I was in the Navy, so I had a problem understanding why we spent so much time learning to march since we would never march around a ship. However, we did not learn to march to look nice in parades, but it was to teach recruits how to listen to and follow instructions. Marching is an extremely effective way to teach these things.

If one marching does not hear the commands instantly and correctly, it will show up immediately. It is embarrassing to be going one way all by yourself when everyone else is going in another direction. Even more disconcerting is causing others around you to stumble or fall because you did not hear correctly. Of course, the trainers want such mistakes to be as humiliating as possible. This is not because they got personal pleasure from embarrassing others, but once we got to the fleet the consequences of not hearing orders correctly and obeying them could cost lives. The bigger or more important a church is, the more costly this inability of people to listen will be.

Getting this kind of training on hearing is rare outside of the military, except in team sports. In team sports, if everyone does not hear the same play being called it can be embarrassing. Worse, it can cause your team to lose. The higher the level you play at, the more serious the consequences will be. Causing your little league team to lose a game is not as serious as causing the loss of the World Series. For this reason, even if one has the best physical qualities for the game being played, the inability to hear and follow instructions will be a major factor determining their real value to the team.

I was recently at a lunch with Coach Joe Gibbs. He led the NFL's Washington Redskins to three Super Bowl titles, making him one of the most successful professional coaches. He won championships as a NASCAR team owner, possibly the only one to win championships in such different sports.

At lunch he talked about how difficult it was to communicate plays to his men on the football field. These were all professionals who had been playing the game virtually their whole lives, but they still had problems getting the signals right. Effective communication is one of the most difficult human endeavors, but it is the one thing that can give a team or military force a huge advantage over their foe.

As I have led multi-faceted organizations for most of my life, I am acutely aware of how rare it is to find people who know how to listen to instructions. The failure to hear and follow instructions has been, by far, the most costly problem I've had. Finding a remedy has been difficult. I have learned to recognize my most valuable people by looking for one's ability to hear accurately and then follow up on instructions quickly, and with a devotion to excellence. With but a couple of exceptions, the only ones I have found who were really good at this were either military trained or had advanced to a high level in team sports. As we get closer to the end of this age, being able to hear and respond quickly and correctly will often mean life or death, and everyone is going to have to have this skill.

Knowing His Voice

Because it is getting more difficult to find people who can hear and follow instructions well, we have devoted a large amount of our efforts in ministry to simply teaching people to know and obey the voice of the Lord. Here is what the Lord said about this in John 10:4, **"And when he brings out his own sheep, he goes before them; and the sheep follow him,**

for they know his voice" (NKJV). We will follow the Lord to the degree we can hear His voice. It is that simple.

Deception is more than just misunderstanding doctrine. Failure to be in God's will is also deception. Even under the Old Covenant, we see the people being repeatedly exhorted to obey His commandments *and* heed His voice. Yet, there are not many Christians who can distinguish the voice of the Lord, even though He says that this is a basic characteristic of His sheep. This is why some of the basic training of Christians needs to be learning to hear His voice.

Many still hold to the doctrine that we no longer need to know the voice of the Lord because we now have the Bible. Really? The Bible itself refutes this incredible belief. The Lord invited His people to reason with Him, which meant He respected their ability to reason. Try applying just reason to the doctrine that God no longer speaks to His people because we now have the Bible. How would any bride feel if on her wedding day the groom told her that he would no longer speak to her personally because he had written a book for her? The quality of a relationship is based on the quality of the communication. What could be more devastating to a relationship than something like this? This is not to detract from the place and purpose of the Bible, but it was never meant to usurp the Lord's personal relationship with His people.

All of God's people must know His voice, not just prophets, pastors, or church leaders. In general, the church is more like a mob than a disciplined army. Not many can hear the commands of the Lord. Many who know He is speaking still cannot understand what He is saying. Often, there is a large disconnect with those who are hearing Him and those who actually obey what He is saying.

Again, knowing the voice of the Lord is not just for prophets or the super spiritual. It is for all believers. Every private in God's army must know His voice and be responsible for obeying Him. Those who grow in this ability to hear are the ones promoted. At times He may speak through them to others. The more we grow, the more we will be able to lead. The foundation is the same for all: **"My sheep hear My voice, and I know them, and they follow Me" (John 10:27 NKJV).**

If we are mostly a mob instead of a disciplined army, with few being able to hear His instructions, how are we going to position ourselves to be a part of His army? There is a clear and biblical step-by-step path to maturity in Christ that we must follow. The following chapters are designed to help get us on the path, moving in the right direction.

The basic law of inertia states that you cannot steer something that is not moving. Regardless of how old we are, or how many years we may have drifted from our purpose, we can still become who we are called to be and do what we are called to do. Nothing is impossible for the One we follow. However, He is the Helper, not the Doer. We must get engaged with the resolve to do all we can to change and be teachable. Just the fact that you would read a book like this shows that you are at least ready to get moving.

Resolve that you will:

1) Know the voice of the Lord so well that you can distinguish it from all other voices in the world.

2) Obey the voice of the Lord with even more zeal than you would obey any earthly king.

3) Keep these two factors as important in your life as food or oxygen.

CHAPTER SIX

Building an Army

As God's people rise up to be the army we are called to be, we must pass through specific phases of growth in order to mature and become effective. Just as civilians do not automatically become excellent soldiers but must first endure the rigors of training, so too do God's people need a systematic process that requires five basic stages.

They are:

1) Mobilizing

2) Teaching

3) Training

4) Equipping

5) Deploying

Each of these stages is critical and must be accomplished in sequence. Only when we have been through all five will we have an effective fighting force ready for the ultimate conflict between light and darkness. Here we will briefly examine each stage.

PHASE 1: Mobilization—Mobilization is the call into the Lord's army. We should hear this call at the time we commit our lives to the Lord. When we accept the salvation of the cross, we have been bought with the blood of the Son, and we are no longer our own, but belong to Him. The call of salvation is individual, and we must each be born again by our own faith in Him, but then we become part of His body, the most important gathering of people there has ever been. His body is also His army.

PHASE 2: Teaching—Once we are mobilized, we must begin the maturing process. Growing up in the knowledge and wisdom of the Lord begins with renewing our minds, conforming our thinking to His. We do this by becoming disciples, studying His Word and allowing the Holy Spirit to "teach us all things" (see John 14:26). This is where we build our biblical worldview, which is learning to see the world as the Lord sees it. As we do this we will also begin to see things in unity with others in the body.

Through the process of renewing the mind, we discover our specific calling and placement in His body, His army. This is a crucial stage in our growth in the Lord. Teaching is an important stage, but we must go beyond it to make an impact.

PHASE 3: Training—Training comes after teaching. It is practicing what we have learned in the teaching stage. At this stage we should have instructors and mentors to ensure proper application of learning, but students must be allowed to grow through the testing of wisdom gleaned through the teaching.

Training prepares the student to be released. When I was a flight instructor, I first taught my students in the classroom about the basic principles of flying a plane. That was the teaching level. Then we got in a plane, and I trained them how to do it. I would first demonstrate a maneuver and then have them take the controls and practice it until they were competent. That is training.

Book knowledge is not enough. How would you like to get in a plane and have the pilot tell you that they have never really flown a plane before, but they've read lots of books about it? Unfortunately, much of the body of Christ is stuck at the teaching level. Multitudes are gathered and taught, but that is not enough. Congregations are often like big sheep pens where the flock is thrown food a couple of times a week, resulting in many well-fed Christians who are bearing little or no fruit for the kingdom.

Jesus did not just teach His disciples. He let them practice what He did, in His presence first, and then He sent them out two by two.

PHASE 4: Equipping—The fourth stage, equipping, is when you receive your weapon. In aviation, for example, you may be assigned to fly a certain plane. In the infantry, you are given a rifle or machine gun. In artillery, you are assigned to a gun and crew on a specific cannon. In the body of Christ we are given divinely powerful weapons like love, truth, and wisdom. In place of guns we have pulpits, books, television, and other media. The weapons of our occupation forces are schools, charities, and missions that reinforce the people in the Lord.

In Ephesians 4, we see that the primary mandate of apostles, prophets, evangelists, pastors, and teachers is to equip the saints to do the work of the ministry. Where can you find this being done today? If there are true apostles, prophets, evangelists, pastors, or teachers leading, you will not find them doing the ministry in a congregation, but rather you will find the saints doing the ministry under their guidance.

PHASE 5: Deployment—The final stage, deployment, is when we get in the fight. This is the commission to ministry with a specific mandate: fulfill our purpose to set the captives free, tear down strongholds of darkness, and prepare the way for the coming of God's kingdom. At this stage, all our prior preparation, trials, and training pays off and is measured in fruit.

Being engaged in a ministry, whether within the church walls or not, is essential for a healthy Christian life. Each member of God's army is uniquely gifted and must be equipped to make an impact in his or her sphere of influence. When we engage in our God-given mission, the life and power of Christ within us is manifested. No matter how old or young, every believer is called to a ministry, and every believer has a mission.

From Boot Camp to Command

Think about the plight of the average new believer in the body of Christ today. They are newborns in the Spirit and require the nurture of mature spiritual mothers and fathers just to survive. Yet, many are left to fend for themselves spiritually from the time they are born again. How many newborn babies in the natural could survive if left to raise themselves? Why then would we think new believers can survive spiritually without help? Alarmingly, only about 5% of those making a decision for Christ are actually added to the church. This is a shocking contrast with the first-century church where 100% of those who came to Christ were plugged into their place in the body, mainly because they were discipled as newborn Christians.

The church, in general, is only accomplishing roughly 5% of its mandated purpose at this time. The other 95% of its time and attention is occupied with things that bear little or no real fruit. The activity and entertainment generated by this 95% may resemble fruit, but simply engaging in activity is not growing up into all things in Christ (see Ephesians 4:15). Gathering people is a start, but it is counterproductive if they are not taught, trained, equipped, and deployed.

In our years of training and equipping the body, our ministry discovered that only a handful of Christians know their ministry or the spiritual gifts they have received to accomplish their mission. Of this group, fewer than half of those were actually engaged in their calling. How well would you be doing if less than 10% of your body was working? That is about how well the body of Christ is currently functioning.

While the current state of the church can be disheartening, there is encouragement. Even with the body operating from such a tiny percentage of its actual ability, it has nevertheless been the most powerful entity impacting culture for centuries. Imagine what the impact will be when the other 90% gets activated.

Military Sequence

As I mentioned before, as a young man I enlisted in the Navy. Immediately, I was sent to basic training where for the first few days we were taught the basics of military life. Then we began serious training under the watchful eyes of instructors.

During those first days, we took a battery of tests that indicated various aptitudes so that we could be placed in a job well suited to our aptitudes. Before we left basic training, we knew what our job was in the fleet. From there, we were either sent to school to develop the skills and knowledge we would need for our jobs, or some went right to the fleet for on-the-job-training. Advanced training was always the next step.

From then on, for the entire time I was in the Navy, I was either in school (I went to several advanced schools), or was training, practicing what I had been taught in a squadron, while always being ready at a moment's notice to actually face combat. We were continually running war games, working out different battle scenarios. As long as you were in the service, you were expected to improve your skills, and evaluations ensured this was the case.

Should this same model not be applied in the body of Christ? In the Navy, we were taught and trained straightaway in basics, and we knew what we were called to do. We continually advanced to higher levels of skill through training, and we never stopped developing our skills. Right after someone is born again, they should likewise be immediately taught and trained in the basics. They need to quickly learn what their mission is and rapidly be set on the path towards teaching, training, and equipping for their calling. Then they must develop a daily resolve to mature and improve at what they are called to do, maintaining this for as long as they are alive on the earth.

Authority and Responsibility

There is a desperate war going on, and the army of God is being mobilized. The war for men's souls is far more crucial than any human conflict in history. The battle has never let up, and those who have eyes to see do battle every day. We do not know how many salvations are dependent on our obedience in God's army. Even the most seemingly obscure ministries may have souls depending on them.

Why is there such a heavy responsibility placed upon us? With the cultural erosion of personal responsibility this may be a hard concept for many to conceive today, but accepting responsibility is the nature of God's call. Consider the consequences of Adam's disobedience. We may think it unfair for others to be affected by our obedience or disobedience. Adam did not ask to be in a position where his actions would affect billions. However, he was given authority over the earth and with authority comes responsibility. The clear teaching of Scripture is that what we do affects others. The greater the authority, the greater the impact will be, for good or bad.

We are not called just to be saved and go to heaven, but rather we have a purpose to fulfill. Like it or not, we are soldiers. We can reject our calling and bury our talents, but we can be sure on that great judgment day we will hear, **"You wicked, lazy slave" (see Matthew 25:26)** if we do.

A major problem in the body today is that many Christians do not have a vital, local church life. These are AWOL (absent without leave). During wartime, AWOL military personnel will either face long prison terms or, if in a war zone, they could be executed. This is because their absence could jeopardize many others. Those in God's army carry that same basic responsibility. We must be engaged and working together to achieve the objective and avoid jeopardizing the ranks.

Granted, many are not engaged in a local church because they cannot find one that is more than the big sheep pen previously described. The teaching they receive from television, books, or DVDs is often better than what they get in a local church. That may be true in some cases, but local church is supposed to provide more than just teaching. There are things the Lord wants His army to learn that can only be gained from the relationships we build in the local body. We must learn to follow the Lord together and become the effective teams we have been called to be.

If we have embraced the cross we no longer have the right to go our own way. We have a calling, a mission. If we are not engaged in at least preparing for that purpose we are AWOL. There is no doubt about the ultimate outcome of this great war we are called to fight, but how we will do in the process, who will be the heroes and the failures, is yet to be decided.

While being part of the Lord's army is a responsibility, it is also an opportunity. You could be used to set many free from bondage, maybe even whole nations. You may not be called to the front line of the battle, but according to biblical standards, those called to behind-the-scenes support will receive as great a reward as those who go to the front.

Marching Orders

Every army has a mission. The most basic mission of the army of God is the Great Commission given to us by our Captain, Jesus, and recorded in Matthew 28:18-20:

"All authority has been given to Me in heaven and on earth.

"Go therefore and make disciples of all the nations, baptizing them in the name of the Father and the Son and the Holy Spirit,

"teaching them to observe all that I commanded you; and lo, I am with you always, even to the end of the age."

Jesus clearly states that all authority has been given to Him in both heaven and earth. This is the key focus of our cause—who has the authority? Our primary goal is to prepare the way for the kingdom of God on earth, for the Lord to take the authority He has been given. We do this by coming under His lordship and stewarding demonstrations of His authority.

The authority the devil is currently exercising over the earth is a usurped authority. It is not the Lord's authority that has been usurped, however, but man's. Dominion over the earth was given to man. The Lord respects this, which is why Jesus had to become a man to reclaim that authority as the Son of Man. Just as Satan, the usurper, does not sit on an earthly throne but uses people to do his will, the Lord likewise exercises His authority through people. The earth was given to man to rule, and the Lord is going to rule over it through man. Now, Jesus has been given all authority over heaven and earth. Even so, His dominion in the earth will not be fully manifested until He returns to reign over the nations and the earth.

Why did the Lord not take His authority over the earth immediately after He was resurrected? Because He knew that the earth's darkness trains His people to use His authority. We are called to rule with Him in the age to come, and the Lord is seeking those who will grow up into Him and walk in His authority.

The first Adam's wife did not care enough about following the Lord's instructions to remain obedient when tempted. Those who are the bride of Christ, the wife of the last Adam, will so value His will that they will pursue it zealously, even against the opposition of hell itself. In so doing, she will be deemed worthy to rule with Christ in the age to come.

Making History

The word "history" is derived from "His-story." As discussed, even with so few of His people actually equipped and engaged, the church has remained a powerful force in world history. So what would the impact be if we took seriously the **"equipping the saints for the work of service, to the building up of** the body of Christ; until we all attain to the unity of the faith, the knowledge of the Son of God, to a mature man, to the measure of the stature which belongs to the fullness of Christ" (see Ephesians 4:12-13)? Is there a church body anywhere in the world that has matured to "**the measure of the stature that belongs to the fullness of Christ**"? Because this is in the Word, we know it will be done. Why not your church? What can you do to help get it there?

CHAPTER SEVEN

The Great Society

Being in God's army is not just about fighting battles. It will be an extraordinary experience of community as well. The comradeship in combat is one of the deepest and unique bonds one can experience. We are being built into a spiritual family that will spend eternity together, so it must be the strongest bond possible.

This bonding together is also a primary spiritual weapon of this force. As Jesus prayed the night before His crucifixion, when His people come into unity the whole world will know that He was sent by the Father. There is a unity coming upon this army like the world has never before witnessed.

Fellowship is a God-given need placed in all people's hearts. The ultimate fellowship is the fellowship of the great. The great ones will be those who have followed the King with a whole heart. The greatest of all will come forth at the end of this age, when all things come to full maturity. As the world's kingdoms collapse and society's foundations crumble, the greatest society of all will be growing on the earth, as we see in Daniel 2.

Common-Unity

The word "community" comes from merging the words "common" and "unity." The army of the Lord will be a community, or place of "common unity," like no other. Every other club or group will pale in comparison to what the body of Christ will soon become. It is often said that when bullets start flying, you are not fighting for your country as much as the person next to you. Those who go through the fire together develop a unique common unity. The same will be true of the army of God.

His warriors will pass through some of the greatest trials together. As we engage in our full mission and become the ministers we are called to be, this bonding will increase like it did for those who gathered to King David. Those who gathered to him were possibly the ultimate motley crew, at least until Jesus gathered the twelve. Yet David's men became the "mighty men of Israel" as they bonded and formed a force together. The Lord's twelve disciples changed the world more than any conqueror.

If you ask someone who was in the military or played sports what they miss most, you will seldom hear that it is the game itself. Rather, it is the team. Being part of the "team" is one of the best parts about being in God's army. There is meant to be a fellowship in the army of God like you will not find elsewhere. It is called *koinonia* in the Greek, and it is a bonding so close that those who are part of it cannot be separated.

Everyone needs friends. Remember, when the Lord made Adam and walked with him daily, God still said it was not good that Adam was alone. Man needed human companionship. Companionship with others is crucial to our spiritual and mental health, and God has provided for His people the absolute best.

The Best Fellowship of All

One of the best characteristics of God's army is that every private has access to a personal relationship with the Commander-in-Chief. In fact, any private could become His best friend. He will share His plans with the lowliest warrior who desires to know His ways. Even better, the lowliest can come boldly into His very throne room at any time and be most welcome.

We can never be fulfilled or at peace in our lives until our relationship with God has been restored. This is the first, highest, and most important relationship we can have. There is nothing as satisfying as our relationship with Him. We were created for this purpose and nothing else can fill the spiritual void. However, He also created us to need each other. There will be a void in our lives without proper human companionship. The army of God is intended to and will be the ultimate human fellowship on the earth because it is also His family.

Defining Family

In these times, the very word "family" does not often inspire positive feeling. Many have experienced dysfunctional and broken families. This is the result of the relentless assault of evil on the family. Because family is the most basic human relationship and is necessary for the health and nurture of people, the devil has been intent on destroying it. His basic strategy is to make bad examples out of as many families as he can, and ultimately, decimate them. He is trying to redefine the family according to his perverted ways. He knows if he can do this in a nation, that nation will crumble.

There is still hope for the family in this time. Scripture says when the enemy comes in like a flood, the Lord will raise up a standard against him (see Isaiah 59:19 NKJV). The body of Christ, which is now riddled with confusion and division, will ultimately be a witness of God's original design for family. Therefore, we can expect the rise of some of the greatest families ever to emerge in the body of Christ.

There is nothing on earth as fulfilling as good family relationships, and this includes connections with our brothers and sisters in Christ. These relationships are not perfect and all families have challenges, but that is the nature of relationships, including those in God's family. Of course, part of our training can include being called away alone for a time to develop a closer relationship to God. Ultimately, however, relationships within a vital local church are essential for our maturity and for our personal families to become what they are called to be, as well. This is the cord of three strands that is not easily broken—our relationship to God, to our families, and then to the body of Christ.

We may have relationships outside of these, such as with co-workers or neighbors, but the three listed above are the most vital for our spiritual lives. Every significant relationship must be cultivated. Relationships do not just happen. We must invest in them if we expect a return. They will be strong and rewarding to the degree we nurture them. Along with our teaching, training, equipping, and in our deployments, this is an underlying factor that is key to accomplishing our purpose. The quality of our unit will depend on the value we put on our relationships and how much we invest in them.

Small is the Next Big

In Matthew 18:20 we are told, **"For where two or three are gathered together in My name, I am there in the midst of them"** **(NKJV).** Recently, my understanding of this verse changed. I once interpreted this to mean that He will be with any group that gathers in His name, even when just two or three are together. Now I think He means for us to just start with two or three. This was a radical thought to me, but now it makes sense. Let me explain.

The key to comprehending Matthew 18:20 is to understand what it means for two or three to "come together" in His name. When you do something in the name of the Lord, you do it by His authority. The "come together" in this verse means more than simply arriving in the same unity of ideas. It means to be "assembled together, bonded." To bond at the depth that the Lord is seeking, we must start with two or three. More than this will make bonding difficult if not impossible. In short, the unity that is coming to the body of Christ is not going to start with large numbers, but with small ones.

Earthly armies also understand the principle of Matthew 18:20. In the military, the infantry is the part of the army that is directly engaged with the enemy. The infantry is built on three-man fire teams. Three or four fire teams make a squad, three or four squads make a platoon, and it grows through the organization of companies, regiments, brigades, corps, and then the entire army. Yet, the basic unit of the army is these three-man teams.

In our ministry, we are applying this principle within our church and the different divisions and missions throughout the organization. We are also encouraging the churches connected to us to pray about one or two other fellowships they can devote their energy and attention to bonding with as fellow members of the body of Christ.

I have been a part of movements seeking to unify the church, but I confess that little, if any, progress has been made as a result. This is not to say that good things did not happen through them, but the main goal, unity in the church, did not happen. Our tactical failure was the result of trying to do it with too many at first.

During the last decade, a common prophetic word I heard traveling throughout the body of Christ was, "Small is the next big." Is this not a call to intentionally start small? We would be more successful if we would apply the lesson of Matthew 18:20, which is to walk together with just one, or at most, two congregations at a time. Then real relationships can be formed, and unity will be established on a deeper level. It will also be easier to discern the Lord moving within our fellowship, keeping our unity based in Him. Once a relationship has a tight, healthy bond, then others can join it without steering the fellowship away from the Lord and His purpose for that group.

If we would seek to begin small and go deeper rather than broader, the strength of the foundation will allow for something significant to be built upon it. This does not negate the value of larger churches and organizations. A mega church coming into unity with another mega church could be powerful. Nonetheless, the greatest and largest movements and churches in history began with a small handful of people, almost always praying. They started strong because they started small enough to be bonded to the Lord first.

The Power of the Few

You may have heard the statement, "The impassioned few will control the neutral masses." This is a historic fact. A tiny percentage of people have controlled the world for good or evil. Consider the following examples.

We have all witnessed a dominant five-year-old child controlling a whole family. A lack of parental authority allows this to happen, often to the spoiled child's detriment and the disintegration of the whole family. The same thing can happen in larger groups and even nations, leading to evil when done with manipulation, intimidation, and threats.

A present example of this in America is the LGBT (lesbian, gay, bi, and transsexual) community's impact on American life.

This tiny percentage of citizens has started to so dominate life in America that virtually the whole world now thinks America has become a homosexual nation. Credible scientific studies have indicated that the homosexual community in America is less than 2% of the population.

The same was true in the early twentieth century Russia, during the time of the Bolshevik Revolution. Less than 1% of the population was Bolshevik, but they were able to take over one of the largest and most populous nations on earth at the time. Marx was right when he said that a tiny percentage of the passionate would rule the multitudes that are indifferent.

The kingdom of God has an even greater example of how it will ultimately fill the earth. The greatest example of unity is the Trinity. The love and unity of the Trinity will be shared with the whole body of Christ, and the world will not have seen anything like this before.

CHAPTER EIGHT

The Battle

The last-day battle between light and darkness is unfolding over various issues and on a number of fronts. However, one battle began so small as to be hardly noticeable, but has grown into a tidal wave—that is the onslaught of the homosexual agenda. Even though this now seems to be the main threat to Christianity in the West, it is not. It is just a symptom of a much deeper corruption and perversion of the heart currently unfolding throughout the world. Even so, because this issue is a present "point of the spear" in the battle for the soul of mankind, we will use it to understand "the schemes of the enemy."

The Agenda

If your first tendency is to just pass over this battle as not important, or not something that you feel called to stand against, then they have been winning with you. This is not about people's sexual preferences; it is basically a battle for our most basic freedoms. However, we are not going to go into this in much depth here, but rather use it to understand the tactics of how the forces of darkness have been winning.

Over thirty years ago, a prophetic friend of mine, Bob Jones, prophesied that Western governments were going to start promoting homosexuality. It sounded too far-fetched at the time, but now it is a reality. How did this happen? They did it slowly, taking small steps. First they co-opted the entertainment industry, then the media, and education. If you take these three, the government will be easy to overcome. It has come to the point that Western nations are viewed as homosexual societies that are so perverting the world that many, such as the Islamic nations, think the only remedy is to utterly destroy Western civilization.

Some are resigned to the meltdown of morality in the West as irreversible, but it is not. We must always keep in mind that the greatest moves of God in Scripture and history almost all came during the times of greatest darkness. This battle specifically against homosexuality is found in the Book of Revelation, and there is no power of darkness that there will not be an ultimate victory over. To understand, we need to look at the principles that are now critical for those who will stand with God, His righteousness, and His justice.

Shutting the "Gates of Hell"

A "gate of hell" is a gate or door through which hell gains entry. The consequences of an open gate of hell can be huge, but it may be a tiny door at first. If we have been in a church for long, we have probably experienced individuals or small groups arising to seek to control the whole body. If the leadership is weak these can be successful in gaining control, often beginning with the smallest issues. When this happens in a family or church, it establishes a bad atmosphere in which no one is happy or at peace, often leading to a break-up of the family, church, or organization. We can even see this kind of thing preceding the division or destruction of a nation.

Right now, in America and Europe, small, ungodly forces have been taking over and controlling the neutral masses. In the last few decades, the high places controlling a culture, such as education, media, government, arts and entertainment, the military, and business have almost all been taken over by forces hostile to Christianity. Some of these forces are hostile to all religions and even to human liberty. Some extreme groups have been quite vocal about their agenda to destroy Christianity, or at least drive Christians underground. Because the majority of the population is indifferent, including most Christians at this time, the agenda of the West is now controlled by a small percentage that is anti-Christian.

Think about what has happened. A few decades ago it was considered almost unthinkable in the West to belittle or attack Christianity. Now it is considered politically incorrect not to attack Christians. We are quickly crossing from what has appeared to be a "post-Christian era" to an "anti-Christian era." This is the nature of the anti-Christ spirit, and it is becoming increasingly effective. However, this will be reversed. Many of these nations that have lost so much moral ground will have revival. This is actually a "pre-Christian era." But this will only happen with an awakening.

The devil always overplays his hand. Ultimately, the sickness and perversion now being forced on Western nations will backfire and that fire will become the greatest revival yet. This process of the creeping erosion of our moral and spiritual foundations can be reversed, which has happened a number of times in history through the revivals and the Great Awakenings.

Flames of Fire

Leonard Ravenhill once told me, "You don't have to advertise a fire." The Word of the Lord is like a fire, and "He makes His messengers flames of fire" (see Hebrews 1:7). Messengers are coming whose hearts are so fired for God that the world will be touched by their heat. Just one of these will put many thousands of their enemies to flight.

In Scripture and in history, we have many examples of just one individual being raised up to turn whole nations to God. One person anointed by God can reverse a thousand years' worth of the devil's work in a moment. All it will take to reverse this is for Christians to not be neutral or lukewarm, but to take their stand as bold, courageous defenders of the faith. Being lukewarm is one of the worst things to happen to a Christian, according to Revelation 3:14-16:

"The Amen, the faithful and true Witness, the Beginning of the creation of God, says this:
'I know your deeds, that you are neither cold nor hot; I

would that you were cold or hot.
'So because you are lukewarm, and neither hot nor cold,
I will spit you out of My mouth.'"

How could anyone who has met the Living God, the
All-Consuming Fire, be lukewarm about Him? If we have
seen the Lord and then become lukewarm, then we have fallen
into the ultimate delusion and deception. There is no greater
affront in a relationship than indifference. Being indifferent
toward God is the greatest insult we could ever give to Him.
Let us resolve to do the opposite, doing all things for the sake
of His gospel as we have been called to do.

To be persecuted is the normal state of Christianity. The
Holy Spirit is the exact opposite of the spirit now trying to
dominate the world. True Christianity tends to make the
greatest advances during times of persecution. Not long ago,
Christians held the high ground in Western culture. What has
been happening in the United States and Europe represents
a dramatic loss of Christian influence, and the belittling
and shaming of the gospel. This also released the growing
lawlessness now dragging an increasing number of souls into
damnation.

This downward spiral into perversion and moral
corruption will be reversed, and the reversal is likely to be
ignited by a few resolute champions of the faith. Keep in mind
that the Lord loves to confound the wise with the simple, and
to confound the strong with the weak, and these few may not
be very impressive in the natural.

We are told in II Corinthians 2:11 not to be ignorant of the devil's schemes. A part of our basic training in the army of God is to learn the tactics of the enemy so we can prevail over them. We will, therefore, spend a little time on this, but there is one strategy of God we want to learn first.

Remembering the principle that a few passionate people will control the multitudes who tend to be neutral—if a tiny percentage of Christians cast off their lukewarm delusions and fall passionately in love with God again, they would begin to infect and wake up other Christians. Then Christians would again become the passionate ones whose influence becomes the salt and light it is called to be.

Love is the most powerful weapon on earth. We are assured that **"love never fails" (see I Corinthians 13:8).** Yet, the majority of the passions that have controlled the neutral masses throughout history have been anything but love. Hatred, fear, racism, pride, and greed, almost every human passion but love, has been in control. Our weapons are different, our methods are different, and our goals are different. As we read in II Corinthians 5:14-15:

For the love of Christ controls us, having concluded this, that one died for all, therefore all died;
and He died for all, so that they who live might no longer live for themselves, but for Him who died and rose again on their behalf.

Consider just how much of our lives, thoughts, actions, and time is controlled by the love of Christ. We should not be as concerned about regaining political influence as we are about reawakening the passion for Christ in our lives. The loss of our first love has caused us to lose the Christian influence in our nation. We must get the fire back. To get that back, we must get our first love back, because only love never quits.

A Different Spirit

As Isaiah declared, God's ways are higher than our ways, and God's love is higher than human love. As we are addressing how the church will take on a military mentality, we need to understand what God's militant love is like. It is not like our human sympathies as many Christians think. Even "tough love" is not an adequate description of it, as we get a glimpse of in Hebrews 12:5-8:

"My son, do not regard lightly the discipline of the Lord, nor faint when you are reproved by Him;

"For those whom the Lord loves He disciplines, and He scourges every son whom He receives."

It is for discipline that you endure; God deals with you as sons; for what son is there whom his father does not discipline?

But if you are without discipline, of which all have become partakers, then you are illegitimate children and not sons.

The Lord is easier on His servants than He is on His sons. He is hard on His sons because He loves them so much. Because of the influence of humanistic philosophies that have perverted modern thinking, this can be a hard concept to grasp for anyone who has not had their mind renewed. We must understand that the hard trials in this life come upon God's people because He loves them, not because He is punishing them. It is for discipline.

Those who enter military combat will be thankful for the toughest drill sergeants. Though they may have hated them in boot camp, once in combat they will quickly realize those sergeants cared enough to prepare them for the world they are facing. So will we when we embrace the Lord's tough training of His army.

One of my best friends is Bart Peacher. His parents were some of my all-time favorite people growing up. They raised me about as much as my own parents. They not only loved their own children, but they loved the other kids in the neighborhood, and the kids loved them back. They were tough, however! What I am about to tell you is extreme, but it had remarkable results for their son, Bart.

Bart was in the kitchen one night lamenting that he had "a learning disability," and therefore could not pass math. His dad replied, "I'll help you with that learning disability." He took off his belt and laid into Bart. Nothing else was done, but after that Bart never got less than a "B" in math. He went on to excel in math and science, got a degree in chemistry, and had a successful career as a chemist. He even became a "Black Belt" in the management system, Six Sigma.

The point is that when we pander to weakness, we only feed the weakness that has people in bondage. Counseling has its place, but I do not think six years of counseling would have accomplished what that one timely whipping did for Bart. That whipping hurt, and probably left some welts that could today land his parents in jail for child abuse, but the real abuse is coming from the unfounded humanistic philosophies that are destroying people. That whipping was done out of love and accomplished far more than many hours of bleeding heart sympathies could ever do. God's ways are higher than our ways, and His compassion is not like our compassion—His works. How is the other working out for us?

We can expect this kind of discipline to come upon the body of Christ to shape it into God's army. Expect the training for God's army to be tough and to go the opposite direction of the training of much of the present Western society, even now in the military. This "tough love" discipline will cause angst and resistance in many. So be it. Every change since the beginning of the Reformation has brought resistance, but the change will come. The same evil spirit behind the emasculation of the West, the kind that creates wimps that can be easily dominated, uses a counterfeit to God's compassion—it is called unsanctified human sympathy, which has nothing to do with true love.

Of course, you can go too far being tough in trying to create toughness in others. No one wants recruits dying in boot camp or on the football field, but we need them to be tough enough not to die needlessly on the battlefield because they were not prepared well.

Because the army of God will be different than any other army, its motivation must also be different. This army cannot be fueled by hatred for its enemies, but rather by love. But it is a true love, not feigned human sympathies. The serious military demeanor that we can expect to come upon the church will be in:

1) Training and preparation for its purpose

2) Discipline

3) Strategic and tactical thinking

4) Actions based on clear objectives

5) Toughness based on caring and resolute devotion to the truth

This transformation to a military demeanor will begin with serious leaders and people with the focused character demanded by the times we are entering. The visionaries will make the changes first, and as usual, they will probably be scorned and ridiculed. That should never surprise us. Troubles tend to focus the senses. They are allowed by our Commander to make us tougher and more sensitive in the right way. Our goal must always be to please the One who enlisted us. We cannot be controlled by what other people think, even some who claim to be His people. We have been at war against darkness of the most desperate kind throughout church history. Many, including most Christians, live as if they are oblivious to this darkness. This will soon change.

Worshipping Warriors

Some of the greatest warriors in Scripture were also the greatest worshippers, just as we see with King David. Worship and warfare go together. Being strong in one of these without the other will lead to imbalance in our lives. Having both in line enables us to endure the hardship of battle without hardening our hearts.

The call that is starting to be heard in these times is II Timothy 2:3-4:

Suffer hardship with me, as a good soldier of Christ Jesus. No soldier in active service entangles himself in the affairs of everyday life, so that he may please the one who enlisted him as a soldier.

A soldier does not enlist in the army because of the great vacations. Though many have become Christians because of the recent emphasis on the promises of health, wealth, or easy solutions to problems, the true soldier enlists for different reasons. They make a commitment to go into harm's way for a cause, and if necessary, to pay the ultimate price for their cause. Soldiers of Christ are called to go even further, resolving to die every day to this world and to live for the sake of the gospel. True Christianity is a life of sacrifice. As we are told in Matthew 16:25, **"For whoever wishes to save his life shall lose it; but whoever loses his life for My sake shall find it."**

When we lay down our lives daily for the sake of the gospel we find fulfillment, peace, and joy far beyond the comprehension of those not following the King. There is no greater liberty than to be Christ's slave. Walking in courage as soldiers of the cross is the path to ultimate freedom—the freedom from fear.

If we have died to this world, then there is nothing this world can do to us. One who is dead does not fear rejection or failure. As a great soldier once said, "A coward dies a thousand deaths, but the courageous only die once." If we die to ourselves and to this world as we are called to do, we will find true life, true freedom, and the path that gets brighter every day, leading to the most wonderful and fulfilling life.

Being a soldier of the cross is both the hardest and the easiest life we could live. It is hard because resisting our selfish old nature is difficult, requiring that we go in a different direction than the world. At the same time, it is easy because living by the new nature, the nature of Christ, is the most wonderful life we could live.

Even so, the true warrior does not serve for the rewards or benefits because it is in their nature to fight for what is right. The Lord is worthy of this devotion. We were bought with the ultimate price—His own life. We now belong to Him. The rewards are greater than any other we could have. As Paul wrote in I Corinthians 7:35, **"And this I say for your own benefit; not to put a restraint upon you, but to promote what is seemly, and to secure undistracted devotion to the Lord."**

One Thing

Mahatma Gandhi's work in India is a demonstration of the power of a focused devotion to Christ and His teachings. Gandhi, while not a confessing Christian, took just one tenant of the Lord's teachings, that of turning the other cheek, into his movement. In so doing, he brought the most powerful empire in the world at the time to its knees and gave birth to a nation. What would happen if someone obeyed two things the Lord taught?

Gandhi was inspired by the writings of Leo Tolstoy. Tolstoy was a Russian Count, a member of the aristocracy in Tsarist Russia, and a great novelist. When Tolstoy encountered Christ he was truly born again, giving away his fortune and all of his land. He lived the rest of his life repairing shoes as a cobbler. He sought simplicity in his earthly affairs so he could contemplate Christ and give himself completely to living according to His teachings.

Because the only example Tolstoy had of institutional Christianity was the Russian Orthodox Church, some of his teachings were a bit reactionary and extreme. He was, however, one of the most interesting and devoted followers of Christ in Russia during the great trauma that led to the Bolshevik Revolution. In the 1970s I studied all of Tolstoy's writings because I had been shown that America would go through a similar trauma and transformation, but it could have a different outcome if we understood the forces seeking to destroy us that Tolstoy helped to illuminate. At that time, it was hard to imagine anything similar to what happened in Russia happening in America, but now the parallels are remarkable.

The United States is in the early stages of another revolution. The outcome will be either a terrible tyranny or a stronger reconnection to the divine wisdom that helped lay our foundations as a nation. At this writing it remains to be seen which way we will go. The forces that would tear us apart are growing stronger. Our national problems are growing beyond human remedy. At the same time there is an awakening beginning. If we turn as a nation back to God, our future will be brighter than ever.

In church history, there are other examples of profound changes that swept over the church and the world as a result of individuals taking a stand for God's truth. Many were tested, often for years, but those who did not give in had an impact that not only changed their generation, but in many cases future generations as well. Truth is a divinely powerful weapon. Those who have it and use it are the most powerful people on earth.

We must prepare for the fact that as the church's light becomes brighter, the more threatened those living in darkness will become. They will attack the church, and Christians must not be caught unprepared. There cannot be a victory without a battle, and the bigger the battle, the greater the victory.

The Prepared

To prepare for the battles ahead, we must not be surprised by any kind of attack. We must realize that God wants us engaged in these battles. Persecution is an indication that God considers you worthy of the kingdom of God, as we read in II Thessalonians 1:4-5:

Therefore, we ourselves speak proudly of you among the churches of God for your perseverance and faith in the midst of all your persecutions and afflictions which you endure.

This is a plain indication of God's righteous judgment so that you may be considered worthy of the kingdom of God, for which indeed you are suffering.

We see here that persecution is God's **"righteous judgment"** so His people could be considered worthy of the kingdom of God. This is why the apostles responded with rejoicing after the Sanhedrin had them flogged. As we see in Acts 5:41, **"So they went on their way from the presence of the Council, rejoicing that they had been considered worthy to suffer shame for His name."**

Pride causes us to do almost anything to avoid shame, but that should be a sure sign that we are not yet dead to this world and alive to Christ. It is a great honor in this life to suffer for the name of the Lord. So much so that it says Moses chose to suffer affliction with the people of God because he esteemed the reproach of Christ as greater riches than all the treasures of Egypt (see Hebrews 11:24-26). Moses turned down the ancient world's greatest wealth for the sake of sharing in the reproach of Christ, yet we often do almost anything to avoid this at all cost. This indicates the level of deception some Christians are under, exposing where their values really lie, esteeming the approval of fallen men more than they do God's approval.

We must have the eyes of the spiritually mature to see true treasure, and persecution suffered in the name of Christ shows us something more valuable than any earthly treasure. Of course, we do not want to provoke people to persecution unnecessarily, but rather let it be the result of living in the light and proclaiming the truth. When persecution comes, we should not only embrace it, but rejoice in it as did the apostles.

Many go to church for comfort and personal encouragement, which is understandable with all of the pressures of daily life. However, those who come just for personal reasons will almost always flee a church that is being persecuted. That is to be expected, but these fail to understand the true comfort and true peace found at the cross. When we lay down our lives, we find them. This is a comfort and peace far beyond what the world can give us. There is no peace like that which comes from knowing that our lives are pleasing to God and we are doing His will.

If we will stop living for ourselves and live for Him as we are commanded, He will give His life to us. That is the best trade we could ever make. If we will fight the good fight of faith and stand for His truth without compromise, He will fight our personal battles, and He never loses. We will not be without personal problems, but for those who have learned to fight spiritually, they know the strength of the Lord's hand. They believe His promise to always lead us in His triumph, and they will therefore endure problems, knowing things will work out for their good.

We are told the whole world lies in the power of the evil one. That means when we are born, we are dropped behind enemy lines. We are surrounded by the enemy at all times. The only way we are going to get out of this is to fight. Let us resolve that we are put here to fight the good fight of faith, which is one of the greatest honors that could be had in all of creation. Let us do it with the excellence and resolve our King deserves.

In the Gospels, the Lord gave Peter the keys of the kingdom because he had the revelation that Jesus was the Christ. The Lord then told him it was upon this rock (the revelation from above of who Jesus is) that He would build His church, and the gates of hell would not prevail against it. The Lord said that the gates of hell would not prevail against the church, singular, not churches, plural. As long as we are divided into churches, instead of being the church unified, the gates of hell will continue to prevail. This is why we are focused here on what we are called to be. If we become that, we will be a force no spiritual stronghold can withstand.

CHAPTER NINE

Anointed to Mobilize

Mobilization is achieved through an anointing to draw people together for a cause. It is not our great personalities or our ability to articulate a vision that actually attracts people to a God-ordained cause. Rather, it is an anointing. Of course, the devil does have a counterfeit anointing to draw people to evil causes, but significant gatherings are supernatural in origin.

As previously covered, mobilizing is the first step in building an army, mission, or organization. There are, however, a few more crucial aspects to mobilizing that we need to understand. How mobilization is done can set the tone and course for everything that follows, so we must get this right.

You can get people to gather by using good marketing techniques, but mobilizing for the Lord's army must be done by the Holy Spirit's anointing. This does not mean we do not use marketing strategies, but we must do so under the anointing and with the dignity and grace of the King.

The anointing to mobilize also applies to numbers. John the Baptist obviously had an anointing to gather great crowds, as all of Judea came out to hear him. However, that does not mean he started out with this anointing to amass large numbers of people. It is likely that John's ministry was not nearly so popular at first. Usually we learn to be faithful in the little before we are given greater authority.

The largest churches, ministries, and movements in the world almost all began with a few people gathering together, usually for prayer. If we have an anointing to mobilize, it will likely begin with a small group of just one or two others, as we discussed in chapter seven. Our faithfulness with little determines how much more authority the Lord will give to us, and it will likely be given in increments. I say this is "likely" because the Lord is sovereign. He does not always do it this way.

Anointing for Numbers

There are some who have an anointing for mobilizing small groups, some for mobilizing hundreds, and some for mobilizing thousands or more. If we would recognize our level of anointing to mobilize, and be able to distinguish this from the level we hope to achieve, it would save us from frustrations and mistakes that scatter people instead of gather them.

We may be called to lead thousands, but there is a difference between the calling of God and the commission from God. We must be content where we are, not losing our vision but resting in the Lord. We are told it takes faith and patience to inherit the promises (see Hebrews 6:12). Faith without patience can be counterproductive. Even though we may ultimately be called to gather thousands, if we presently only have an anointing to gather a couple of hundred, then an annoying pressure is placed on people when we try to go beyond that current level. It can draw people for a time, but they will not likely remain long.

If God has called you to pastor three hundred, then you can use all kinds of promotions to try to grow your congregation beyond this number, but you will eventually fall right back to three hundred people. The reverse is also true. If you have been called to lead five thousand, church splits or other problems may temporarily shrink your congregation, but it will eventually return to five thousand.

If we are faithful with little, He will, at the proper time, give us more authority and anointing to gather. We want to be sure He is the one promoting us. Gaining influence that God has not yet called us to will always bring problems that a wise person would want to avoid. The issue is obedience. It is much better to be a brilliant and effective lieutenant than an incompetent general.

Pruning for Power

In John 6, the Lord preached a message that was intended to thin out the crowd, removing those who had selfish motives from those really wanting to follow Him. This chapter marked a major demarcation point in the Lord's ministry. After John 6, the crowds following Jesus seem to get smaller rather than bigger. Previously, the Lord's ministry focused mostly on the multitudes. After this point, He seemed to concentrate on His disciples. Before this chapter, He did miracles so the people would believe. After it, He only did them for those who did believe.

The point is that just because the crowds are bigger does not mean the ministry is more important. In fact, biblical examples show that the truly mature ministries of the Lord are far more given to disciples than crowds. This is seen with the Levite priests who ministered to the nation until they were fifty years old, at which point they became elders who sat in the gates. The few disciples the Lord concentrated the latter half of ministry on would go on to accomplish much more than the masses that followed Him. Could we be sensitive to a change like this in our own lives and ministries?

Think about Philip, who stirred the entire city of Samaria. The Lord told him to leave and go speak to one man in the desert. How many of us would have thought that word was from the Lord? Philip obeyed, and though he may not have known it during his lifetime, centuries later when missionaries made it to Ethiopia, they found a nation that already believed in Jesus. That may have been more fruit than was ever realized from the revival in Samaria.

We were faced with a similar choice a few years ago. One of MorningStar's missions is to host conferences. Most of our conferences are devoted to equipping people in specific ministries or gifts of the Spirit. We have been able to gather thousands, and it seemed the trend was toward increasingly bigger gatherings. Then we were given an option of gathering large numbers and generally spreading encouragement or gathering smaller groups—those who would be high-impact leaders in the future. We chose the latter and moved to hosting smaller equipping conferences for those intent on doing the works, not just seeing them demonstrated.

Our ministry has gotten smaller in some ways, but we are now reaching far more people as a whole. We've produced videos that were viewed by more people daily for a time than all of the news networks combined. Many of our short publications go viral, and our books continue to be distributed around the world. We could have used the mindshare and timeshare to produce large gatherings instead, but I don't think we would be bearing nearly as much fruit for the kingdom.

We can host a dozen smaller equipping conferences with the same effort it took to plan a large one. Actually we are hosting more people per year with the many smaller gatherings than we were with the bigger ones. The people are just spread out over more conferences. The depth of impact we see now is much greater. We may not know until eternity, but I believe the fruit of our ministry has multiplied since we made this change to focus on smaller gatherings. However, it is not about the size, but about doing the will of the Lord.

The Source of Anointing

Adolf Hitler had an anointing from the devil to mobilize people. The German people who followed him were some of the most brilliant, educated, and cultured in the world. After the devastation of World War II, many Germans commented that they did not understand Hitler's command over them. Some said they actually disliked him and his politics, but when they heard his speeches, all doubts about him faded. His speeches were not impressive in either content or delivery. In fact, his voice was borderline irritating. The people were mesmerized, however. His sway over them was called supernatural by some, and it was.

On the Allied side in World War II, General Eisenhower had a similar ability to mobilize, but with a different spirit. Most thought he was likeable, but not impressive. When British Prime Minister Winston Churchill reviewed his plan for the D-Day invasion, it was so complex that the Prime Minister did not think it had any possibility of success. Eisenhower's demeanor and faith in the resourcefulness of his troops was so compelling, however, that Churchill began to question his own doubts. Later, he remarked that he did not understand what happened, but something came over him to trust the General.

Combating Confusion

Combat soldiers often remark how confusion is one of the most dominant factors in combat. Confusion is actually prevalent in most conflicts, and it takes a true leader to keep the initiative and necessary aggression through it. In most combat situations the day will usually be won by the most decisive.

Because confusion and uncertainty is so prevalent in the world, anyone with confidence in where they are going will inspire courage in others. Courage is basic to any advancement or accomplishment, and imparting courage in the midst of confusion is basic to leadership.

Having clear direction and imparting courage is even more important for spiritual leadership. Spiritual leadership does not have the kind of motivation a business leader has by offering a paycheck, or a military leader's advantage with their rank. The power of spiritual leadership is based on vision, character, and most of all, the anointing. Those who follow will only do so if they believe in your calling from God, your vision, and your ability to accomplish that vision.

Another factor in spiritual leadership is that the people's confidence in their human leaders must eventually be replaced by confidence in God. This is the ideal, but you cannot force this transition too quickly or it will not work. Most people need to follow a human leader at least for a time. In John 10, we are told His sheep know His voice and follow Him. However, it does not say that His lambs know His voice. Lambs follow other sheep until they mature and come to know their shepherd's voice for themselves.

Maturity of the army of God will be determined by how well every soldier comes to know His voice and how well they are resolved to follow Him. However, if our training and equipping is done well, they will need human leadership less and less because they know the Leader's voice.

D-Day was more than just an extremely important day in modern history—it was unique and remarkable in a number of ways. Eisenhower and his staff greatly contributed to the success of that day by putting together plans that placed forces on the beaches and directed them where to go. However, the day was won by young junior officers who made on-the-spot decisions and took initiative, sometimes making decisions that were far above their pay grade. The troops, in at least some degree of confusion, rallied to the courage of those who seemed to know where they were going, and this won the day.

In contrast, Hitler so micromanaged his armies that even his generals were afraid to make minor decisions without first consulting him. It could take hours for communication to go to Berlin and back, and by the time Hitler's commands got back to the army, they were no longer relevant to the fast changing situation. The difference in these two types of leadership was a main factor that led to Allied victory.

Likewise, our goal as leaders should not be to teach people to obey us, but rather to hear the Lord for themselves and to respond to His will decisively. Of course, the Lord speaks through His leaders, but every one of His people is required to know His voice because there will be times when leaders cannot be found.

Decision Fatigue

Another major factor in the German army's communication breakdown could have been because Hitler had to deal with so many minor issues, causing him "decision fatigue." At times, he seemed to zone out and could not make a decision when one was badly needed. It is now known that most people can only make a few high quality decisions a day without beginning to suffer this fatigue. This is why "micromanagers" almost always end up as major failures.

The Lord does not seem to be a "micromanager." In Scripture we see that the more mature a leader was, the less direction they seemed to get from the Lord. He did not lead His apostles around by the hand, but rather He sent them. They made a decision, and if correction was needed He would give them a dream or revelation. For the most part, however, they were mature enough to be trusted with most of the decision making. It is the immature who, like young children, need constant instruction.

If the leadership in the church does its job well, the people will continue on without missing a step regardless of what happens to their leaders. Isn't that what happened when the church was persecuted and driven from Jerusalem? The people took initiative and started preaching the gospel everywhere they went. The goal of spiritual authority is not to establish our authority over the people, but rather the Lord's authority over them. Our mandate is not to make them our own disciples, but His.

The Greatest Human Leader

Jesus said John the Baptist was the greatest man born of a woman. What made him great was he prepared the way for the Lord. This remains true of all the greatest leaders. They prepare the people to know and follow the Lord. Like John, they are happy to decrease as He increases.

John had an extraordinary anointing for mobilizing. Scripture says that "all of Judea" came out to John (see Mark 1:5). He did not dress for power and/or seem to have good manners. He had chosen the Jordan River valley as his place of ministry, which is close to the lowest place on earth. There was no reason in the natural for the people to gather to him, and it can only be explained by one thing—John had the anointing to mobilize.

Why did God give John this anointing to mobilize? John operated in time and alignment with His purpose, and the Lord knew he would use the anointing rightly. He used it to prepare the way for the Lord, to point to Him, and then he got out of the way. This is still the greatest purpose of true ministry—to prepare the people for Him, and then be willing to get out of the way.

Counterproductive Mobilizing

Even with a true anointing to gather, we must not assemble God's people just because we can. When people come together without a clear purpose or for a selfish motive, it will likely result in confusion and scattering rather than building and gathering, as we see in Acts 19. Then, when we try to mobilize, we will find it harder and probably have a far smaller response. It is a serious matter to take people's time and resources when God is not behind it.

Mobilizing does not accomplish much without training, equipping, and deploying to tear down enemy strongholds and set captives free. Gathering large groups of people is not hard with good promotional techniques, but what is actually being accomplished? What is the fruit? Does the fruit remain and continue growing?

Being able to gather God's people is important, but it is also a major responsibility. We must always keep in mind that these are His sons and daughters. If they are gathering to us, it is not because of us. If we are all they are presented with, then they are being cheated. Did the Lord really call the gathering? If we are not gathered together with two or three to see the Lord in our purpose, we could be wasting our anointing. It is somewhat like a bank account. We will be quickly overdrawn if we do not put in more than we are trying to take out.

Managing mobilization can be diverse and complicated. The greatest gatherings will soon be upon us as multitudes pour into the kingdom. The Lord wants those gathered added to the church, not lost. This will only happen if those with an anointing to gather multitudes learn to partner with those who can teach, train, and equip them for their purpose.

Again, these are not just crowds, these are sons and daughters of the King. Managing something of this magnitude is beyond any church organization or human ability. That is why we must know the Lord as the Head of His body. He upholds the universe with His Word, and we cannot do it without Him.

A friend of mine, Brad McClendon, recently had a prophetic experience. He saw the Lord sitting on His throne with all of His leaders gathered before Him. The Lord was sharing things about Himself, but only a small number of the leaders were listening to Him because it seemed too basic. They were trying to look past Him to see the things that were about to come on the earth. When these things came upon the earth, only the small group who had actually listened to the Lord tell about Himself were prepared for them.

Jesus does not just have the answer to every human problem, He is the Answer. He does not just give us guidance, He is our Guide. Now is the time to prepare for what is coming, and we do this by getting to know Him. As we are told in Psalm 32:6:

Therefore, let everyone who is godly pray to You in a time when You may be found; surely in a flood of great waters they will not reach Him.

The foolish wait until revival breaks out to get ready. The wise do not waste time but rather prepare now. The wise also know if something happens too quickly or too easily, it is because it is insignificant. If He delays, it is because the Lord is giving us more time to get ready. He is likely doing this because we need it.

CHAPTER TEN

Kingdom Administrators

A s previously discussed, a wise leader will discern the level of their anointing and stay within its bounds. To go beyond our level of anointing is to step outside the grace we have been given to lead. This puts us in the place where our own strength is required to hold together those whom we have gathered. This is the point where many go awry, using manipulation, control, and hype to keep the people. Leaders who fall into this trap are using a spirit other than the Holy Spirit to do the work. This is always counterproductive and will ultimately result in scattering the people.

"God resists the proud, but gives grace to the humble," **(see James 4:6, I Peter 5:5 NKJV).** It is pride to think we can go beyond the grace God has presently given to us. This is the root of the pride that caused the first fall, and most falls since. Once when I felt crushed under the weight of trying to save the world, I had an encounter with the Lord. He reminded me

He has already saved the world. If I worked myself to death trying to do His work, then it would be counted as a suicide, not martyrdom. Because I am a slow learner, I still get ahead of Him at times and this always results in a lot of hard work that later must be undone.

In Psalm 46:10, the Lord commands us to **"Cease striving and know that I am God."** If we really know Him as God, we will cease striving and trust Him. This creates a resting in Him that is required for doing His work. He said that if we would take His yoke, we would find rest for our souls (see Matthew 11:29). You do not put a yoke on when going to bed, but when going to work. When we work yoked with Him, we actually find refreshment for our souls. That is why He said His work is easy and His burden is light (see Matthew 11:30).

Now many are ambitious to reach large numbers because they know God desires for all to be saved and come to the knowledge of the truth. These are seeking to be successful for His sake. Ambition is not wrong, but selfish ambition is. Staying within our anointing and grace is not just about numbers. The best spiritual leaders are the most committed followers of Christ. Ultimately, this is about following the Spirit of God. Only by doing this will we truly be doing His work. Many activities may appear as good, but if they are not His work they will not last.

In leadership and management, there is a concept called "The Peter Principle." This is basically going beyond one's grace and ability. This principle states that organizations tend to promote people to their level of incompetence. It is often true that people are effective until they get promoted beyond their level of ability. Then, these previously effective people can become a bottleneck in the system, hindering further progress.

One way we try to guard against The Peter Principle is by employing and promoting people on a trial basis. We are clear with each new hire or promotion that it is a trial basis, and we give them a timeframe for evaluation before we make the position permanent. Although it is always difficult to tell people they did not pass the trial period, it is ultimately less problematic than if that person had stayed in a position for which they were not capable. This would ultimately hurt them and probably everyone else in the organization, and even those served by the organization.

Levels of Ministry

The anointing for mobilizing specific numbers discussed in the previous chapter also applies for preachers or teachers. One can be a remarkable teacher of a group of hundreds, but cannot hold the attention of thousands. When I first became aware of this reality, I would watch a church leader with a congregation of three hundred people speak to an audience of thousands. I noticed that with the larger audience, almost exactly three hundred people seemed in tune with the message. The rest would disconnect. This was not about the content of the message, or the delivery, but it was about the level of anointing.

These things I have come to understand from observations and personal experience I consider principles, not laws. Principles have exceptions, and I have seen exceptions to the above. For a long time it was hard for me to understand why someone with a great anointing when speaking to the smaller groups, and who tended to have great depth and timeliness to their messages, could fail to connect to a bigger crowd. This was in spite of the fact that their leadership skills were often better, sometimes even more advanced than the people leading large groups. Why is this?

One reason may be that when the Lord walked the earth, His greatest works and deepest teachings were given to small groups. He did not walk on the water in front of everyone, just His disciples. He still seems to prefer doing His greatest miracles with the fewest witnesses. Could it be that the Lord esteems the small gatherings as more important? After all, He did call His followers a **"little flock" (see Luke 12:32).**

This concept often offends the sensibility of those seeking great numbers, but it may be true. The early church met in the temple with a large crowd, and they also met from house to house, which of course would have been smaller gatherings. Some of the most effective churches have had the wisdom to adopt both types, holding larger meetings but also having small groups for those who want to go deeper.

Three is the Number

The Lord had a ministry to the multitudes, but it seemed that He gave far more attention to His closest disciples. Then He had the twelve with whom He went much deeper and invested more time. Then He had three,

Peter, James, and John, with whom He shared everything. Healthy, balanced ministries tend to have relationships on all three levels.

The tabernacle of Moses and the temple were also divided into three sections: the Outer Court for the multitude, the Holy Place for a few ministers, and then the Holy of Holies where only one could go. Having different levels of ministry is not discrimination, though the immature or insecure might consider it as such. It is simply necessary for the building of an effective church, ministry, or organization.

Without a clear path to maturity for Christians, discouragement will eventually set in, along with the tendency to become lukewarm. There are worse problems than feeling left out from the inner circle. You are not discriminating if the path is open to everyone, but there must be standards of maturity required for advancement, or the whole process is "dumbed down" to a level that lacks the challenge we need to grow.

We must heed the Lord's warning when He said, **"Woe to those . . . who are nursing babies in those days" (see Matthew 24:19).** We could interpret that as, "Woe to those who keep their people in immaturity." Without challenges and new levels to attain, people will remain immature.

Discriminate

It is a delicate matter to discuss levels in ministry. This can create an opening for a wrong type of discrimination and stereotyping, but godly discrimination, also known as discernment, is sometimes necessary for growth in the body. Everyone discriminates to a degree, regardless of whether they are aware they are doing it. The right use of discrimination helps those who are the most in need. For example, when you keep an infant away from a table where tough meat is being served, which could choke them, you discriminate for their safety. Even worse would be to serve everyone baby food because you do not want to offend the babies.

Discrimination, as godly discernment, can be a good thing when used rightly, and it is essential when organizing a group for a specific purpose. In the military, they begin basic training by separating the people gifted in one area from those gifted in another area. For example, when going through flight training, a person may be brilliant and possess great multi-tasking ability, but if they are prone to motion sickness they get discriminated against and washed out. This is done not only for their sake, but also for the safety of the others being trained and the nation they will be defending. They may have great multi-tasking ability, but it will be greatly hindered when they are airsick.

Likewise, effective intercessory prayer groups should learn to discriminate against some not truly devoted to prayer and who cause disruptions. We may offend them by disinviting them to the intercession, but that is better than offending everyone else because they don't want to come because of this person.

In our MorningStar prophetic teams, a team member must demonstrate both a prophetic gift and a certain amount of maturity before being accepted into the team. If we failed to discriminate and opened the teams to anyone, they would quickly lose their ability function properly. So it is with every other team. Even with sports teams, any member that becomes disruptive is cut.

Discriminate Forward

In the Lord, discrimination is based on competence, but also heart issues, such as faith, patience, courage, endurance, and above all, love. You may have great knowledge, intelligence, and wisdom, but without these heart issues, you will be a poor leader in His kingdom.

Vision casting is a primary key to mobilization. What greater vision is there than to grow up into Christ? The Lord made it clear that the path to fulfillment is taking up our crosses daily—living for Him and not ourselves. He told us we must humble ourselves to be exalted, and we must die to live. This is the cost of true discipleship, but it is worth the cost.

It is currently estimated that the majority of Christians in the United States are no longer part of a local church. They have left the fellowship of their local body for various reasons, but many of these reasons would not exist if a clear path for spiritual advancement was provided and standards maintained for those who advance. When people are not challenged toward maturity, frustrations begin to take root.

As Scripture makes clear, anyone can be as close to the Lord as they want to be. Enoch, for example, was so close to the Lord that He took him directly to heaven. Nowhere does it say we cannot have that experience. Neither does the Bible suggest that we cannot be a better prophet than Isaiah, Elijah, or John the Baptist. In fact, we are all called to go beyond what they walked in and actually become like Jesus, doing greater works than He did. Jesus provided the opening to go as far and high as we want. His church should reflect this opportunity.

In 1982, I was told that the most effective leaders of the future church were going to come from professional sports. This was because these leaders were learning things in sports that were essential for a vital church life, but the church was not teaching or practicing them. These things related to training, knowing your place, teamwork, and performance evaluation for determining who got in the game. In sports those who sit on the bench may be frustrated, but the kind you want on your team will use this to get motivated to rise to the level where they do get in the game. If we keep dumbing down the standards to make everyone feel included there will soon be no motivation for anyone to improve.

Spiritual competition can open a door for evil, but when it calls others to a higher standard it can be used for good. The Apostle Paul referred to the Christian life in terms of running a race. You do not run a race against yourself. We are also warned about comparing ourselves to others. This is true when it leads to jealousy, and though we want to keep the Lord as our standard, and the One we are growing up into, it is not wrong to be inspired by others who are operating on a level above us if it motivates us to grow.

Multi-level Principles

In 1989, I was told that people in multi-level marketing businesses understood vital kingdom principles better than the church. This amazed me, but I quickly began to understand what He meant. In multi-level marketing you only prosper as you help others prosper. In that system, you actually hope recruits outshine you. The same is true in Christ. Our rewards will be based on the others we have helped, those whom Paul calls "our crown" (see I Thessalonians 2:19).

I once asked a highly successful multi-level marketer the reason for his success. He replied that in his particular system everyone knew how high they could advance, they knew where they were, and they knew the next step to advancement. Basically, the path to advancement was clear and practical. This is an important kingdom truth that much of the church is missing, and the Scriptures suggest it is necessary for our maturity in Christ.

In Scripture, we find five basic levels of maturity in Christ:

1) Believer

2) Disciple

3) Servant

4) Friend

5) Son

There is a biblical description for each of these levels, with a progression from one to the next. Interestingly, some people read their Bibles many times and do not see this progression, while others see it immediately. Maybe it is related to our level of devotion, or simply that the Holy Spirit waits to reveal this truth until a certain time. We can still progress through these levels without seeing them. Just as we may not know everything about electricity we can turn the switch on. It would be easier if we did see them, however, and were more intentional about our spiritual growth. Again, we are as close to the Lord as we want to be. How close do we want to be?

CHAPTER ELEVEN

Getting Stronger

I n Proverbs 4:18, we are told, **"the path of the righteous is like the light of dawn, that shines brighter and brighter until the full day."** If we are on the path of the righteous, or the right path, it should become increasingly clear and our lives continually brighter. In the last chapter we began to address how creating a clear path for maturity and spiritual advancement is important for motivating those who have been mobilized. We will continue that discussion here, but take it deeper.

The path of the righteous is made clear in the Scriptures, but motivation and diligence are required to search it out. The Lord does not hide His ways from us, but He hides them for us. Thomas Paine said, "What we obtain too cheap, we esteem too lightly." It is only by seeking His will with a whole heart that His ways will be valued as they deserve. Devotion to the Lord must be the primary focus of our lives if we are going to stay on the path of life.

Our salvation was freely given to us, but it was not without cost. It was bought at a cost greater than all the world's treasures—by the blood of the Son of God. By His sacrifice Jesus purchased us. We are no longer our own, but belong to Him who alone could pay this price. As we see in the Book of Revelation, Jesus is still called "The Lamb of God" in honor of what He did on the cross. We dishonor what deserves the greatest honor when we behave as if our salvation was cheap. It is freely given to us, but as a gift of great value, and it should be treated as such.

While we are freely given salvation, the Scriptures are clear that our eternal position and rewards are earned. The Apostle Paul, possibly the greatest missionary apostle of all time, wrote near the end of his life that he did not consider that he had yet attained to the high calling of God in Christ (see Philippians 3:12-14). Paul was not talking about eternal life, which he received the day he believed in the atonement of the cross. Rather, he was speaking of a calling so high that even after a remarkable life of devotion and service he continued to press on towards that calling. This high calling is available to those who are similarly devoted and diligent in running this race.

This theme is also seen in Jesus' parable of the wise and unwise virgins. To be careful means to be full-of-care. If we care enough for the anointing of the Holy Spirit, we will steward it and keep our lamps full of the anointing by pursuing Him above anything else. True love will always be diligent and focused on following the Lord, becoming like Him, and doing His works.

Because you are reading this type of book, you are clearly motivated to advance farther than the average believer. In fact, you are in a group that probably contains less than 10% of all Christians. We cannot blame the present lukewarm state of the church on leadership and religious systems alone, yet these surely bear some responsibility for the careless spirit of the times. To be careless means to care-less. Nevertheless, this lukewarm condition is an opportunity for the diligent to stand out. This is likely why the believers in the lukewarm church of Laodicea were given the greatest reward for overcoming. Who will be of a different spirit than the spirit now prevailing over much of the church?

There is no cause nobler than the cause of Christ. When believers declare this truth through the faithfulness of their lives, the more motivated passive Christians will be to rise to the great cause. Proverbs 29:18 states, **"Where there is no vision, the people perish" (KJV).** Christians will die spiritually without a vision. Vision casting is a crucial part of leadership, but clear instructions for accomplishing the vision must be included.

Words of Life

Soon after we become Christians, we should have a vision of how far we can go in the Lord. Our basic calling is to be like Him and to do the works that He did. Christ lifted the bar even higher by declaring we could do greater works in His name. We can be as close to the Lord as anyone in Scripture. In fact, their stories are recorded to encourage us to pursue the closest relationship with Him. If we seek Him, we will find Him. If we draw near to Him, He promises to draw near to us. How close to Him do you want to be?

After developing a vision for drawing close to the Lord, a most important element is to establish the path to maturity and spiritual advancement. This path should be clear enough to be understood and followed. This too is what proper leadership provides. I call this the Ezekiel 37 commission.

From Dry Bones to an Army

In chapter 37, Ezekiel was shown a valley of dry bones. By the Word of the Lord he began prophesying to these bones until they came together. He kept prophesying until life came into them, and they became an exceedingly great army. One of the callings of the prophetic ministry is to see in even the driest bones an exceedingly great army, and then prophesy to those bones until they come into their destiny.

The motivated are easily led, but a higher form of leadership is to inspire "dry bones." You do not have to be a prophet to see how dry and disconnected the body of Christ is now. Who has the words of life to call those parts together as the "exceedingly great army"? Where is the leadership that can gather the discouraged and disconnected, mobilizing them with vision and purpose?

Ezekiel 37 was a primary motivation for forming prophetic teams at MorningStar. We have been blessed with some of the most devoted, on-fire Christians as members of our local church who do not need much motivation. However, we all become dry and/or atrophied if we are not doing the work of the Lord. For this reason we have put together many ministry teams to be sent into some of the driest nations and denominations.

This required a new level of prophetic maturity for many of them. We learned, however, that the driest wood ignites the fastest. Something that would be hardly noticed in our local church could be a spark that starts a great fire in the parched ones. Those who have learned this now get more excited the drier a place is that they are sent to. For this reason, we should not lament the dry state of the church in our nation, but see it as the opportunity that it is.

Many want to see great miracles, but they don't want to be put in the place where they need one. We tend to see the greatest miracles where there is the greatest need. We must not just criticize the church for its current state, but rather seek words that will help her become what she is called to be.

We also have our own dry and difficult times. The wilderness is part of the journey to the Promised Land. In the wilderness, Israel built God a dwelling place and had some of their greatest experiences with Him. We need a vision for using the dry times, seeing them as the opportunities they are. Adopting this perspective would probably get most of us through the wilderness quicker.

A main devotion of the rising prophetic ministry in our times is to impart the ability to see others as they are called to be, not as they are now. That is a major reason why people from around the world visit our services almost every week to receive prophetic ministry. These people are desperate to hear from God about their purpose, and those who serve on these teams have true prophetic gifts from God to help them.

Dead Dry

We do not want to give up on people or churches because they are dry. Yet, no Christian is called to be dry. We are called to have a river of living water flowing from our heart that can never be quenched. We can be in arid places but not be dry. We need to be a source of living water for those who are thirsty.

That being said, we have all met people who thought themselves better than others when in fact they were the driest, deadest of all. Those like this are trapped in a religious spirit like the Pharisees. There may be exceptions, but in general, a subtle form of pride is the root of this condition.

This came to my attention when many of these "dry ones" would seemingly boast that they never go to conferences or travel to find the Lord because He is with them where they are. That is an understandable belief, but there are some biblical challenges to that mentality.

Of course, the Lord is always with us, and all of God's people should be able to hear Him for themselves. Likewise, our personal rather than corporate relationship to Him should always be the most fulfilling. This does not mean, however, that we do not need others. There is a reason why the Lord commanded all of Israel to go up to Jerusalem three times a year and gather before Him. These meetings were not the primary source of their relationship with the Lord, but they were still crucial to their spiritual development.

There is a dynamic when we "go" that simply does not happen when we stay in our usual, comfortable place. The healthiest Christians I know are those who try to make several conferences or gatherings a year. They are also the most fruitful workers in local congregations because they are constantly enthused with vision and life.

Certainly the Lord can speak to us where we are, but as we see in Scripture, the Lord did not often do this. Those who do not value His Word enough to go and seek usually do not find. Biblical kings, even those like David who were prophets themselves, had the wisdom and humility to seek a word from other prophets. At times they traveled great distances to seek a word. At that time traveling long distances was difficult and expensive, but they esteemed His word that much.

Why does the Lord seem to make seeking Him difficult? What makes something a treasure is that it is either rare or hard to find. His words, His wisdom, and the knowledge of His ways are the most valuable treasure we could find on this earth. Who could ever put a value on anything higher than a word from God?

We have seen thousands of lives changed because of the devotion of those seeking Him to travel great distances. We know that the level of anointing we and our prophetic teams have is not from us being spiritual as much as it is the hunger of those coming. Only the famished seek food and only the thirsty will search for a drink, and the Lord promises to feed the hungry and satisfy the thirst of those who seek Him.

Perhaps this is why the great army now being formed will be largely comprised of dry bones that were desperate enough to search for Him. These are the ones who will be so thankful when they find what they seek that they will be willing to fight the good fight of faith to keep it.

Maybe this is why the Lord had all of Israel go up to Jerusalem three times a year to celebrate His feasts. Perhaps this is why He chose to pour out His Spirit on the Day of Pentecost when Jerusalem was filled with sojourners. He richly rewards those who will make a great effort to seek Him.

Certainly we should have our most fulfilling relationship with the Lord at home and within our local church bodies, but there is a traveling factor to our faith as well. Those who have learned this tend have the richest of spiritual lives. Those who travel to other places to worship the Lord have their vision constantly expanded by experiencing new people, movements, and the ways of God. This seems to be a major factor keeping people from becoming lukewarm or old wineskins. In my experience, almost every person who told me that they did not need to leave their comfort zone to find the Lord had all of the characteristics of an old wineskin.

The Builders

Earlier we discussed the presence of an anointing for mobilizing different sized groups. Some things are accomplished best in large groups, and some things are accomplished best in small groups. In the kingdom groups of all sizes have their place, but some things are accomplished better within a certain size group.

For example, apostolic level teaching is usually better for a large group, which is why the apostles in the first-century Jerusalem church taught in the temple. There is a type of corporate worship that flows well within large meetings, which may be why the worship in heaven is conducted with myriads of angels. Vision casting is also better done in a large group.

In contrast, such levels as personal ministry, equipping, and training are more effective in a smaller group. Missionary teams, for example, can become cumbersome if they are too large. Therefore, when we are seeking to mobilize people we need to consider the purpose and then select the proper group size. With every group, regardless of the size, we should discern the strengths and weaknesses to better prepare the members for their purpose.

We must always keep in mind how the Lord loves diversity and moving in unique ways. During a MorningStar board meeting, Bishop Wellington Boone once shared that a great weakness of Pentecostal and Charismatic circles was their devotion to topical rather than systematic teaching. This is true, and I would add that a great weakness in non-Pentecostal and non-Charismatic churches is the devotion to systematic teaching rather than topical preaching. We need both for a healthy church, recognizing when and how to use each. We need to be free to have times to stay at home and seek Him, but we also need to know when it is time to go.

Building People

Studies have shown that the number one question people have is what is their purpose. Building healthy congregations means promoting both a common vision for the group and a personal vision for individuals. Each person needs to see how they fit into the bigger purpose, but they cannot know this without also knowing their own unique purpose.

Many years ago, I heard a great teacher say that most churches are not temples made of living stones. Rather, they are piles of living stones that have not yet been built into something. This is why so many Christians get easily displaced from a church or ministry. They have not been cemented into their place.

Many do well at building projects and ministry outreaches, but it is rare to find one who truly builds people. When the apostolic ministry is restored to the church builders of people will become preeminent. Consequently, local churches will become far more stable and powerful. When everyone knows their place and are cemented there, it will take a lot to pry them out again. You can steal stones from a pile, but try stealing one that has been concreted into a building.

A builder's mentality is different from that of a teacher or mobilizer. Occasionally they are found in the same person, but this is rare. Thus, true New Testament ministry is a team ministry. Some must gather like Philip did in Samaria, and others must follow that work and build, as the apostles Peter and John did in this case. In these times there are many who can gather great crowds, but not many who are spiritual master builders, as apostles are called.

When we first planted our church in the Charlotte area, Steve Thompson asked me what I envisioned for this church. That was a good question. I told him that until I saw the building materials the Lord would send us, I did not know what the church would look like. Having been a builder for a time, I understood how to build with different materials. A wood-framed house is built differently than a brick house. You need different skills, tools, and materials for each. Building a true habitation for God with people makes it crucial to make our plans around the materials we have been sent.

This does not mean, however, that we build everything around what people want. Rather, our plans are based upon what the Lord indicates when He sends us the materials with which to build. These materials are usually what the people need, not necessarily what they want. We must be wary of trying to fit every church into one vision or pattern. Again, God loves diversity. The seven churches in Revelation were all different and needed a personal word from Him, even though they all existed in the same region at the same time.

As I expected, the Lord sent mostly prophetic and artistically gifted people to our church. What I did not expect was how few pastors arrived. People gifted in the prophetic and the arts are often wounded, and none of our original team members were very good at helping hurting people. To the shock of some, I would occasionally announce that people who needed spiritual healing should consider going to another church. I knew there were congregations in our city better able to help these people. As their shepherd, I considered it my responsibility to see they received the best help.

A number of people took my advice and sought help in other congregations. Many of these were outstanding people, and I hated to see them go, but once they were healed they became great gifts to these churches. In this way we were able to seed extraordinary people into other churches and all benefited. Many are still friends that we see occasionally. We must ultimately remain true to our goal of building the kingdom, not just our congregations.

If we have building materials that are a better fit elsewhere, I try to gently get them to consider other congregations. While I do not want them to feel rejected, I want the Holy Spirit to be completely free to place people in the body where it pleases Him. If some come who do not fit with what we are currently doing, I also consider that the Holy Spirit may have plans beyond what has yet been revealed to me. We must all keep growing. Even biology teaches that any living thing which stops growing starts dying.

The Greatest Builders

If a spiritual builder has done their job well, the people under their influence will have their identity in Christ more than in their profession, culture, race, or nationality. They will know their calling and will have the opportunity to develop it. If you ask them what they do, their first thought would be what they do spiritually, their ministry, not their profession.

The church is called to be like a city set on a hill, brightly lit so as to capture the attention of all around. There is a call to be the great society, representing the kingdom of God on earth.

We are also called to be a beacon of hope for goodness, truth, healing, redemption, and restoration. God's army is to be an irresistible force for righteousness and justice.

Even though there does not seem to be many who have eyes to see this great city of God, it is forming now. Like Abraham, the true sojourners are seeking this city, and they are finding their place in it.

CHAPTER TWELVE

Quality of Force

After mobilizing, the speed and efficiency of training will have the biggest impact on the quality of the force. Presently, there are few churches that are equipping the saints to do the work of the ministry as described in Ephesians 4. Most are devoted to preaching and teaching, but there is little training of the people to walk in their own ministries and gifts. Though this church model is virtually the only one used now, we can expect this to change for thosel that will be relevant in the emerging times.

Those who do not make this basic change will not likely survive much longer. Concerning the times at the end of this age the Lord warned, "Woe to those who nurse babes" (see Matthew 24:19). As previously discussed, we can interpret this as "Woe to those who keep their people in immaturity." Not equipping the people to do the ministry as stated in Ephesians 4 is possibly the main factor keeping God's people in immaturity. If we do not equip the people to do the ministry, then we are not really one of those equipping ministries listed in Ephesians 4. This change must be made. In this chapter we will begin to examine some practical ways this will happen.

Orientation

First, we should be thankful for the great preachers and teachers in the body of Christ. We have been blessed with some of the best. Now we must follow up the teaching with training, equipping, and then deploying those who have been equipped. At the same time we do not want to discontinue the great preaching and teaching, but rather see it enhanced and expanded. We're not doing away with these, but adding to them.

Even if people are well taught, trained, and equipped, they will atrophy fast if they cannot use their gifts and ministries. There is ample opportunity for this, especially where the great harvests are now taking place. As I am writing this, an associate ministry just had an evangelistic campaign in Karachi, Pakistan, and nearly 300,000 new believers committed to follow Christ. These are in need of teachers who will help establish them in sound doctrine so they become true disciples, not just converts. They are in need of pastors, prophets, and apostles to ground them in the fellowship of the body of Christ that is essential for Christian maturity. There are campaigns like this happening continuously now, and few of these have much follow up. This must change, and we have plenty of people resources for this change.

The Rules of Life

People naturally respond to needs from the place of their identity and calling. In America, for example, we have about eight times more lawyers than the average nation. Lawyers naturally think the answer to a problem is a new law, new rules. Because of this, we are an increasingly legalistic society where rules are piled on top of rules for just about everything. Even Christians are taught mostly principles in place of the first-century apostolic message of Christ and the resurrection.

Some of these principles can be helpful or needed, but you can teach a parrot to say and do the right things that are not in its heart. The ultimate work of the Lord is to change hearts. When that is accomplished, people will do the right things because it is in their nature, not simply because they know the rules. Leaders do not think like lawyers. Leaders respond to a problem with leadership, taking the initiative to lead through it. We are called to follow the Lamb, not rules and formulas.

The Easy Path

It has been said that preaching something is ten times easier than doing it. If that is true, and I think it is, we could say that listening to a sermon is probably a hundred times easier than living it. The work of transformation may begin with teaching, but that is only the beginning. If teaching is not followed by training, equipping, and deploying, we fail to really accomplish much, regardless of the sermon's power or depth.

There are few ministry schools or seminaries that actually train and equip their students. Most seminary and Bible school programs are based on students listening to lectures by preachers and teachers. Rarely do the students get to even practice preaching or teaching, much less the real work of the ministry. Thus, if they become pastors, they simply model what they learned at seminary—that it's all about teaching or preaching, not training.

I have heard many great messages preached. On occasion I have asked people listening to the same message what they thought of it. If they agree that it was a great message, I ask them what the main points were that made it great for them. Rarely has anyone been able to give me even one point. They would say something like, "It was the encouragement in it...." They loved it and got excited, but somehow they did not process it well enough to even remember the main points, much less do anything with it. Encouragement is important, but what is that accomplishing alone?

We obviously have a breakdown of attention spans today. The increasing inability of people to focus is being blamed on television, computers, and all the new gadgets, but regardless of the cause, there is an increasing inability of people to actually hear and remember what is being said. There is an even greater inability to actually engage with the truth to apply it to our life. This can and will be overcome, but right now this is a serious problem that not much is being done about. The military has a different and very effective approach to this issue that we need to consider implementing.

Bearing Fruit

Before digging down into the military approach to this a little deeper, consider the Lord's teaching in the Parable of the Sower. Those who are the good soil hear the word so that it takes deep root in them. They then cultivate the seed and watch over it until it matures and bears fruit. Who are these in the church? They are the rare souls who listen, take notes, and go home and review what they learned. They pray over it and keep the seed watered. They will daily review it to see if it is growing in their life, cultivating their hearts to keep the weeds out that would choke the seed (the cares and worries of this world). These are the ones who will bear fruit, some thirty, some sixty, and some a hundredfold. How many do you know who are so faithful? There are some, but they are rare.

If the preachers and teachers have such a hard time doing what they are preaching and teaching (and most of us do), how much harder will it be for those who heard one message to apply it? Studies have shown that repetition is required for retention of a fact or truth, which is why I try to sow a lot of repetition into my messages and books. It will take more than this, however. Training must follow teaching. Training is what helps the word really take root in our life. Training is more than telling someone what to do— it is showing them how to do it and then coaching them as they try. Training requires watching them as they practice, giving advice and corrections as needed, as the Lord did with His disciples.

Knowledge without application can be dangerous. Experience turns knowledge into wisdom. That is why the Lord did not just teach His disciples, He trained them, releasing them very quickly into doing the ministry.

The Path to Power

Power is the ability to accomplish something. In Luke 10, Jesus sent His disciples two by two to preach the gospel, heal the sick, and cast out demons. That is amazing trust, but it becomes more remarkable in Luke 11. In that passage the disciples asked Him to teach them to pray. This suggests that He sent them out to preach before they knew how to pray. That is how fast Jesus had His disciples doing the work of the ministry. Where can you find this today? We will never have the results Jesus did until we start doing things His way. We can agree that no one will ever prepare disciples better than Jesus, so why do we not follow His example?

Starting Poorly

In one of our staff meetings, Steve Thompson once said, "Anything worth doing is worth doing poorly." Everyone thought he was joking, but he was not, and he was right. When representing the King of kings we want to strive for excellence because of Who it is we're serving and the importance of His work. However, there must be a place for starting where we are and growing through experience. What great musician plays their first song perfectly? They all started poorly, making terrible noises instead of music. The greatest artist probably began by drawing stick figures.

When we first start preaching, we are not going to be like John the Baptist. Guess what? Neither was he! He likely started out stumbling like every one of us. If he had not been given the chance to learn from mistakes, God's people would fail to become all they were meant to be.

Until we start fulfilling the basic mandate in Ephesians 4, we need to question if we are in fact building churches or just franchises. As we discussed, we have found that less than 10% of Christians know their purpose in Christ, and even fewer are functioning in their calling. That's how well the body of Christ is doing right now. The encouragement is that the body of Christ worldwide is accomplishing so much, even in this terrible condition. When the whole body is functioning, there will have never been a force on the earth like the body of Christ.

The School of the Spirit

Good training requires a safe place for people to learn from mistakes without being condemned, or hurting themselves or others. In the late 1980s we began School of the Spirit (SOS) services on the model of providing a safe place for God's people to try their wings in ministry, and to be able to make mistakes without hurting themselves or others. As we honored those who made mistakes for having the faith to step out, the atmosphere lightened up, and in this comfortable setting people started trying to fly. Most had a few crashes, but they learned to fly and got stronger and stronger.

I was expecting chaos at some of our SOS meetings and was not disappointed. That is when I probably said for the first time, "We may die of a lot of things, but boredom won't be one of them!" There was hardly a meeting when I did not want to beat my head up against a wall at some point. And there was hardly a meeting when we did not leave in awe at the great things the Lord had done. Proverbs 14:4 says, **"Where no oxen**

are the manger is clean, but much revenue comes by the strength of the ox." So, we resolved to keep big shovels nearby and continue. Just the freedom of those meetings drew people from all over.

To my surprise, the chaos in some of these meetings seemed to release the Holy Spirit in greater measure at first. In Genesis 1 we see that the Spirit moved upon the chaos, and look at the beautiful creation He brought forth. He seems to thrive in chaos. He does not leave you in it, but He knows how to deal with it and loves the opportunity. In our disaster response missions we discovered that the more chaos in a disaster, the more likely the Spirit was to move. Don't be afraid of a little disorder, because He is not. He is a God of order, and He knows how to bring order out of chaos.

Cleaning up a mess now and then was well worth the effort in our SOS meetings. We tried to honor mistakes by commending people for having the kind of great faith required to try something so stupid. We laughed a lot and yelped a lot. It's not that we did not take the Lord's work seriously, but we knew we could not take ourselves too seriously. A liberating atmosphere was created, and people who had remained in the background started stepping out. Many of those became fruitful members of our ministry teams. Some have gone on to become powerful leaders of churches and ministries that are having an impact.

We also resolved that we would call mistakes "mistakes" and stupid things "stupid." We did not want to devalue the Holy Spirit by calling something good that was not, but we also encouraged anyone who was trying to keep going. This worked. When the Lord moved in a truly great way, He often did it through people who had made the most embarrassing mistakes when first trying. Those who stumbled had at least one thing going for them—they obviously pleased the Lord because they had enough faith to step out. We are told faith pleases the Lord (see Hebrews 11:6). To get back up after a mistake or failure can be the greatest faith of all. Those who did this were rewarded, and we learned a great deal about how the Lord prepares His chosen vessels.

Did the Lord not choose the most unusual people for His leaders when He walked the earth? They remained pretty edgy, too. They were radicals and revolutionaries to the end. Throughout church history this has been the case for those who have had the greatest impact. It will also be the case at the end of the age when some of the greatest works of God ever will be done on the earth.

Changing History

At one time, both Hitler and Stalin considered becoming priests. How could history have been changed if their extraordinary gifts for leadership had been used in the church? Think about the possibilities of armies of light, truth, and healing marching across Europe instead of the destructive ones that did ultimately march. The church has a long history of rejecting people and things that the devil then takes and uses for great evil. It seems the enemy saw the potential in both Hitler and Stalin and gave them a chance after the church rejected them.

Of course, we need to consider that the church discerned the seeds of evil within these men and rightly rejected them for that reason. Personally, even if I saw the potential for evil in them I would have at least tried to get them saved and transformed. As deep as the devil has his roots into someone is how deep Christ can fill them when the evil is removed. That's one reason why our weaknesses become our strengths in Him.

The Lord gave His church authority to release on earth what is released in heaven (the spiritual realm). Could the church's tendency to abort potentially great gifts and ministries have contributed to the release of a spirit of abortion in the times? Could much of the evil that we are now facing be the result of the church not helping those with great potential for good or evil?

Anointing or Annoying

If we are representing Almighty God, the most compelling Being there is or will ever be, the church would never be boring. It is dull because we have allowed the religious spirit more influence than the Holy Spirit. The religious spirit has much of the church tied in knots, afraid to make a mistake or offend someone. We cannot follow Jesus if we are controlled by fear instead of faith. If we follow Jesus, whose words and actions constantly offended someone, we will do the same.

What we release in the heavens will get released on the earth, as evidenced by the religious spirit's dominance over much of the earth in the form of political correctness, or PC. Some might protest that the PC police are mostly agnostics or atheists, but unbelievers can be the most devout promoters of this religious spirit. The Bible makes it clear that if we are not offending people and being persecuted, we are not living righteously. If we are controlled by the PC police, we are obeying the religious spirit instead of the Holy Spirit.

Life is Messy

If our view of church life is clean, neat, and in perfect order, then we need to read the New Testament again. Consider the Lord's own meetings. Often demons cried out, and people would throw themselves into the fire. Others would cut holes in the roof to let those in who needed prayer down to Jesus. Girls with less than stellar reputations would drench Him in perfume, and so on. Then, He had those who were the embodiment of the religious spirit of the times, the Pharisees, challenging everything He said or did. This sounds more interesting to me than the typical church of today.

John Wimber once told me how a group of theologians were questioning things that were manifesting in The Vineyard movement. He assured them he never allowed anything in his meetings that was not found in the New Testament. When this seemed to appease the theologians, John asked if they had ever read the New Testament.

I was in a number of Wimber's meetings when demon-possessed people would cry out and begin thrashing about, sending people and chairs in all directions. John, and the people, always took it in stride, cast the demon out of the person, and then went on with the meeting as if nothing had happened. When I asked the Lord why so many demon-possessed people came to John's church, He said that He did not have anywhere else to send them to get them free. It caused chaos at times, but it was worth it. It was also actually very exciting. Many churches could use more demon-possessed people coming to them (just for the practice and the excitement).

I visited many Vineyard churches over a couple of years in the late 1980s. I don't remember one where every member was not trained in praying for the sick and casting out demons. Even in John's meetings, when a demon manifested in someone, it was the people sitting closest that usually cast it out of the person. Then they would lead the person out of the room for more ministry. John would just watch from the pulpit until the people had taken care of it and then carry on with his message.

I have not had much interchange with The Vineyard movement since John passed away, and I've heard that it is very different now. However, at least for a time there may not have ever been a movement that was fulfilling the Ephesians 4 mandate to equip the people to do the work of the ministry as well as The Vineyard.

Seeking order and neatness is not wrong, but an over devotion to it can cause us to snuff out life. Life is messy. When the Holy Spirit moves it can look chaotic for a time, but this is the result of the chaos in people's hearts being released so they can be changed, delivered, or healed.

The spiritual descendants of the Pharisees will be offended by every true move of God, just as they were when God Himself came and walked among them. The greater things that He did, the more they were offended. When He moves through His people today, the "spiritual Pharisees" will behave the same way. The greater the Lord moves through you, the more critics will try to snuff it out. If you want to continue in an authentic move of God, you must resist the Pharisees of our time just like Jesus did.

That does not mean that everything done in a move of God is His Spirit. In true revival people get free, and when people are first free they can sometimes go a bit too far. They will sometimes do silly or embarrassing things. This comes with the territory. To stay in an authentic move of God you will have to resolve to be embarrassed at times. I think He allows this to weed out those who care more about what people think than what He thinks. We must be more concerned that the Lord is free to touch people than about our reputation with the spiritual Pharisees.

Just as the Lord Jesus called everyday people as His leaders and workers, He does the same every time He moves in a new way. He has not changed, and He still trusts the common people more than He does theologians and religious professionals. I say this being a theologian and religious professional. Those of us who are can also take heart that the Lord also called Saul of Tarsus, the "Pharisee of Pharisees," and made him into a pretty good apostle.

However, without question, the Lord obviously prefers to call the most common people to be His leaders. Because the Lord chooses His leaders this way, they are almost all going to be on a long learning curve. They may do awesome things and then follow them with stupid actions, just as we see throughout the Gospels and the Book of Acts. The Lord never seems to be made uncomfortable by His people's mistakes, and no blunder was beyond His ability to fix. He obviously loves real life and people being genuine.

I have watched a number of people go from being unknowns to building significant ministries. In almost every case the ones who grew the fastest and went the farthest were those who started with the biggest mistakes. I think this is why the Lord gave the keys of the kingdom to Peter. Peter made some serious errors, but he also had some of the greatest accomplishments. Even his most terrible mistake, denying the Lord, did not stop him. He repented, got back up, and kept going. This is the nature of true faith—Peter's confidence was not in himself, or his faith, but in the Lord.

Church history has followed this trend. The highest standard of excellence is a worthy goal, but to get there we will likely have to embrace much that is far from perfect. If it is worth doing, it is worth starting out doing it poorly. Even the great Apostle Paul was not the great Apostle Paul when he began his ministry. Rather, he was an immature apostle like all apostles were when they started. If we want the best gifts, we must be willing to clean up the biggest messes. If you want a clean stall, you are going to have an empty stall. Our goal must be to see in an immature Saul of Tarsus a great apostle Paul, and then help him get there.

Staying on Course

In Romans 1, we are taught that we have been given a conscience and the ability to follow or disregard it. The resolve to follow our conscience, or what we perceive to be right or wrong, is the basis for character. Character is strengthened by good teaching and training. This is why we have teaching and study as basic Christian disciplines. The better the teaching and study, the more disciplined the people will tend to be.

Of course, there are exceptions. Some amazingly disciplined people who have the highest character have had little teaching or training in discipline or character. We can likewise find some undisciplined people who have had the best teaching and training. Even so, generally the superiority of a person's character will be affected by the quality of the teaching and training they have received. This is a crucial element in preparation for the times when all character will be tested.

The Power of Practice

In Matthew 13:52 the Lord said,

"Therefore every scribe who has become a disciple of the kingdom of heaven is like a head of a household, who brings out of his treasure things new and old."

Some of our greatest treasure is the truth we have been given. It is the spiritual food and water that keeps us alive spiritually. Just as every meal is not expected to be completely original, your staple diet will be foods you are familiar with and eat over and over. The same is true spiritually. This is why we read the Bible continuously, but also other books and materials that can help us.

We need new revelation and understanding constantly as we grow in the Lord. We also must let what we already know continually flow through us to keep us alive and on track. A pastor once said that his wife had prepared him thousands of meals, and only a handful were so outstanding that he remembered them specifically. Yet, all the other meals kept him alive. Therefore, the repetition of sound doctrine is essential for spiritual health just as the repeated eating of natural food is necessary for our bodies. Occasional surprises may help keep our diet interesting, but it is the exception, not the rule.

If you enjoy watching team sports, you will often hear coaches interviewed before a game equate their chances of winning by the quality of their team's practices. Every coach knows that the quality of practices usually determines the quality of their team's performance during the game. The most successful teams focus their practices on the fundamentals of their sport. The most successful athletes and other professionals will almost always be those who know and practice the fundamentals.

One reason why I like to go to professional golf tournaments is because they give you access to the practice range and putting greens so you can watch the pros practice. It is inspiring to see this. They have a multitude of ways to make practicing the basics interesting. Every day of our life is our practice, and the Lord helps to make them infinitely interesting by making every day different. How different would our lives be if we took every day as seriously as professional athletes do their practice? Embrace life and resolve to never waste a trial and never waste a day.

Even though PGA golfers are so creative in making practices interesting, they are amazingly serious when they practice. Several years ago, I was watching two of the best-known golfers at the time on the putting green and noticed that they were betting on each putt. They were not doing this because they were addicted to gambling, or cared about winning the little bit of money they were competing for, but it was to motivate them to make every practice putt count. They are that serious because in a tournament a single put can mean hundreds of thousands of dollars.

Occasionally, I have spoken to professional football teams before games. Their focus and pre-game preparation are so intense that they can be scary. Once, when I was speaking to the Denver Broncos, I heard the Lord say to me that when I saw the same kind of resolve and focus, or "game faces," on His people, then the kingdom would be near. I have never forgotten that, and I look at every crowd I speak to in order to gauge their focus. Lately, I have begun to see this kind of focused resolve and seriousness in some. We are getting closer.

Every Christian is called to run a race for a much greater prize than a Super Bowl trophy. A single soul is worth more than any sports championship. When we wake up to the prize we are running after the focus will result in a faith that will move mountains.

General Patton was considered one of the greatest field commanders in World War II. He attributed his victories to the high level of training he gave his men. His men did not like him or his fierce discipline—until they got into battle. They were so prepared and disciplined that it opened up strategies other commanders had never considered, because their men could not have carried them out. During the Battle of the Bulge, Patton's army accomplished what the other commanders considered impossible. This great general almost never credited his victories to strategy, but rather to the training of his men. The great leaders we can expect to emerge for the army of God will be like this.

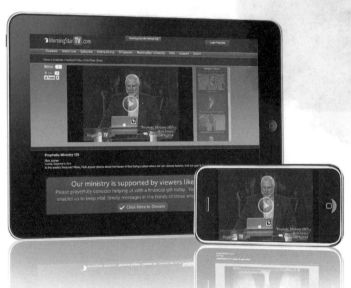

COMMITTED TO THE BELIEF THAT THE LOCAL CHURCH IS SUPPOSED TO BE **THE TRUE SCHOOL OF MINISTRY.**

In recent polls, less than 5% of people in an average congregation know what their gifts or callings are and only about 2% of those are actually equipped and functioning in their calling. **What body could possibly live if only 2% of its members were functioning? MSU exists to fulfill God's purpose for Christ-followers, the local church, and the body of Christ.**

MORNINGSTAR UNIVERSITY

For more information or to apply, visit:
MorningStarUniversity.com

MorningStar
PARTNERS
— WORKING TOGETHER IN THE HARVEST —

The most powerful spiritual force since the first century is mobilizing. We are looking at the greatest potential impact for the gospel ever seen. We need Partners to help raise up and send the most high-impact ministries in church history.

Join with us to equip the body of Christ through our schools, missions, conferences, television shows, and publications. Your contributions are used to train and equip all ages in their prophetic gifting. You can become a MorningStar Partner with a regular contribution of any amount, whether it is once a month or once a year.

Partnership Benefits:
- Receive monthly newsletters with rich, timely content from Rick Joyner and others
- Participate in live video webinars featuring key prophetic voices
- Connect with Partners and staff at exclusive Partner events and in our Koinonia Lounge
- Enjoy a complimentary subscription to the MorningStar Journal
- Save money with special discounts on products, hotel rooms, conferences, and more

Partner With Us Today:

MStarPartners.org

Or Call 1-803-547-8495